LOVE
Never
Ends

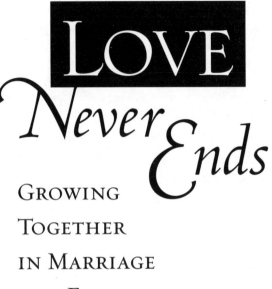

LOVE
Never Ends

GROWING
TOGETHER
IN MARRIAGE
AND FAITH

ROBERT H. LAUER
AND
JEANETTE C. LAUER

UPPER
ROOM BOOKS®
NASHVILLE

Cover Design: Ed Maksimowicz
Cover Photo: Masterfile
Interior Design and Typesetting: Pam Mullins and Nancy J. Cole
First Printing: 2002

Library of Congress Cataloging-in-Publication Data
Lauer, Jeanette C.
  Love never ends: growing together in marriage and faith /
Jeanette C. Lauer and Robert H. Lauer.
     p.   cm.
ISBN 0-8358-0949-8 (alk. paper)
1. Marriage—Religious aspects—Christianity. I. Lauer, Robert H. II. Title.
BV835 .L357 2002
248.8'44—dc21

                                                              2002002057

To those growing with us
in the love that never ends:

Jon, Kathy, Julie, Jeffrey, Kate,
Jeff, Krista, Benjamin, David,
and John Robert

OTHER BOOKS BY ROBERT AND JEANETTE LAUER

CONTENTS

PREFACE

A threefold cord is not quickly broken.

—Ecclesiastes 4:12

The metaphor of a threefold cord captures the essence of Christian marriage. It depicts a strong marriage where God, husband, and wife are securely entwined. In such a marriage, partners nurture each other's faith. As their faith deepens, their marital bond becomes further strengthened.

This book explores the reciprocal relationship between marital and spiritual growth. Growth is rarely quick or easy. Therefore, we do not anticipate that this book will be a "quick read." We urge you to take time to study the book together as a couple. You might take turns reading a section or chapter aloud to each other. Or each of you might read a section or chapter before talking about it together. Allowing sufficient time for discussion is important.

We have included a "Face-to-Face" section at the end of every chapter to aid your discussions. Each section contains exercises designed to cultivate your relationship and your faith by bringing you face-to-face with your spouse and with God. We suggest that you keep a couple's journal to make the best use of the exercises. A couple's journal serves as a record of your shared journey in intimacy. It will include points on which you differ as well as those on which you agree. In essence, your couple's journal tells the story of your marriage in all its intricacies and uniqueness. It is both a tool of intimacy and a record of a shared spiritual adventure. Write in your couple's journal both spouses' responses to the "Face-to-Face" exercises as well as your thoughts on other materials in each chapter.

Does all this discussing and journaling sound like a lot of work? If so, we remind you of two things. First, Paul admonished each of us to "work out your own salvation with fear and trembling" (Phil. 2:12). The Greek word translated "work out" means to work at something in order to achieve or bring about an outcome. In other words, keep working at a task until you complete it. If the task is building a strong, meaningful marriage and developing a vibrant, effective faith, you never quite finish. Room to grow always remains.

Second, the lifelong task of building your relationship and your faith does not mean you are doomed to endless drudgery. On the contrary, the rewards will accumulate. The same letter to the Philippians in which Paul called us to work out our salvation has been called the apostle's letter of joy. Over and over again in that letter, Paul spoke of joy and rejoicing. Indeed, any increment of growth that you experience as a Christian and as a couple will most certainly bring a measure of joy to your life.

We expect and pray that your journey through this book will be an adventure in joyous growth.

I would have to say that these are the
best times of our life together.
Our marriage is better than ever.
Happier than ever.
What a gift from a loving God!

—Bryan, reflecting on his marriage of fifty years

1

God's Gift of Marriage

Then the Lord God said, "It is not good that the man should be alone; I will make him a helper as his partner."

... Therefore a man leaves his father and his mother and clings to his wife, and they become one flesh.

—Genesis 2:18, 24

Several years ago, we asked people to share their experiences of joy with us. In the more than one thousand responses we received in this study, people mentioned relationships, including marriage, most frequently as their source of joy. Colleen, thirty-four years old and married for seven years, kept returning to her marriage relationship when she talked about joy:

I love being with Sean. I feel twinges of joy when I see him after work. I feel joy when he does things or says things to let me know that he loves me. I feel joy when I remember moments we've shared in the past. You know, looking back over our time together, I feel I really came alive when I met Sean.

God created vital, life-giving marriage. At the dawn of time, God spoke the cosmos into existence, not with a single command but in stages. It seems as if God paused and examined each stage, rejoicing in its goodness and completeness before proceeding further. When God created man, God saw that everything in creation was good, but still creation was incomplete. God observed, "It is not good that the man should be alone" (Gen. 2:18). So God created woman and gave to humans the sacred gift of marriage.

MARRIAGE IS A SACRED GIFT

Like the heavens and the earth and everything therein, marriage expresses both the Creator's goodness and the goodness of creation. God gave us marriage because it is a significant source of fulfillment. To be sure, many persons find fulfillment in the single life. A few find their needs realized in the solitary life. Most people, however, seek fulfillment in marriage.

To label marriage as God's sacred gift does not ignore the destructive nature of some unions. As with all of God's gifts, humans have a knack for misusing, misunderstanding, and falling short of God's intentions. Even successful marriages endure times of struggle and disappointment. Such times may not be enjoyable; but they may be, at least in retrospect, times of growth.

In theory, if not always in practice, marriage in all its aspects is good, designed by God for human fulfillment. The goodness of marriage can be seen in its potential to satisfy many of our basic needs and concerns:

1. *Marriage helps fulfill the need for intimacy.* Intimacy—a close, personal relationship with at least one other person—is a basic human need. Evidence is overwhelming that humans do not thrive without intimacy. We know that without warm, human contact, babies can die even if they receive sufficient food. And adults who lack intimate relationships suffer the emotional pain of loneliness—pain so intense that it often leads to physical illness. At every stage of life, humans not only hunger for but also need meaningful connections with others. God has given us marriage as a primary vehicle for meeting this need. In marriage we can love, be loved, and nurture the next generation in life-giving intimacy.

2. *Marriage provides a healthy context for expressing sexuality.* God created us with a powerful sex drive and a basic need to express our sexuality. God also gave marriage as the ideal context for sexual activity. First of all, it's a healthy context. A gynecologist told a woman friend of ours who has been married for thirty years: "One of the best things you have done for your health is to have sex with only one man during your life." The number of people afflicted with sexually transmitted diseases

reminds us that we have healthy and unhealthy ways to express sexuality. It is no exaggeration to say that marriage is God's way of offering us protection against the ravages of promiscuity.

More important, marriage provides the context for greater sexual intimacy. In marriage, sex is more than just a physical act. It is an emotional and spiritual act of loving and sharing between two committed individuals with a history of meaningful experiences. Physically becoming "one flesh"—the special connectedness of marriage—furnishes the opportunity to find sexual fulfillment with a partner you love and trust and with whom you are creating a unique life experience.

3. *Marriage fosters higher levels of physical and mental health.*[1] Health surveys indicate that more married than single people rate themselves as "very happy" and that married people have lower rates than do single people of maladies such as alcoholism, physical health problems, and emotional illnesses. The fact that marriage offers an effective buffer against the various stresses of living is another reason it is "not good" for humans to be alone.

4. *Marriage enhances individual creativity and skills in the art of living.* How do you cope with a tyrannical boss? How do you deal with a neighbor whose children keep running through your flower garden? How do you structure your time and conserve your energy so that you can meet the demands of life? The old adage "Two heads are better than one" applies to such common challenges. Two minds are more likely than one to generate

creative solutions. Two people are more likely than one person to possess all the requisite skills for abundant living.

In this regard, God's observation in Genesis 2:18 is interesting: "I will make him a helper as his partner." "A helper as his partner" translates the Hebrew *'ezer*. The Hebrew scriptures often use this word to describe God's relationship to humans. In other words, woman will be a "helper" in the sense that God is a helper. The word *helper* exalts the role of woman and reinforces the idea that a man and a woman united in marriage form a far more powerful unit for meeting the challenges of life than does either person separately.

5. *Marriage addresses the need for new experiences.* We heard a psychiatrist identify a problem as the "trauma of eventlessness," referring to a situation in which people suffer from insufficient stimuli. While we do not thrive in chaos, neither do we thrive in deadly sameness. Marriage offers endless opportunities for new experiences from birthing and raising children to sharing interests, hobbies, and travel. In effective marriages, partners encourage each other to try new things and spur each other on to new adventures.

Hear what one wife had to say:

> I tend to get stuck in the routine of living. My husband is just the opposite. He likes to venture out and try new things. He has expanded my world in a way that would never have happened otherwise. I have eaten foods, gone places, and attended shows I would have never experienced on my own. And I love it.

6. *Marriage creates a family atmosphere in which children are well nurtured.* One of the best gifts a couple can give their children is a happy and healthy marriage. Children raised in single-parent homes are more likely than those from two-parent homes to have problems with health, adjustment at school, and relationships with peers. They are more likely to get involved in delinquent behavior, including the use and abuse of drugs. We say that they are "more likely," not that they are doomed to this behavior. Yet who wants to increase the chances, however small, of such things happening to his or her children? Again, we see God's wisdom in creating marriage.

7. *Marriage facilitates spiritual growth.* As a husband told us, "My love for God and the love I give to and receive from my wife are so intertwined that it's hard to separate them in my mind. She has been as important to my spiritual growth as she has to my other needs." This husband would tell you that faith has been the foundation of his marriage. But he is saying more than this—marriage has also been vital to the growth of his faith.

We often hear couples mention strong, shared faith as one of the most important factors in the vitality and stability of their marriage. It is equally true that marriage can make an important contribution to a growing faith. In contrast to one strand of thought in Christian history, we do not believe that those who remain single have a spiritual advantage over those who marry. To be sure, the celibate, single person may devote all of his or her life to growing in grace and serving God. But that person is not necessarily purer or holier than the individual who chooses to marry.

Marriage is not inherently less compatible than the single life with spiritual growth. The notion that Mary, the mother of Jesus, remained a virgin and had no other children assumes that such a state somehow reflects godliness more than a typical married life. Madeleine L'Engle, reflecting on the issue, affirms that Mary was a virgin at the time of Jesus' birth. But she adds,

> Then, I hope, Mary and Joseph were able to fulfill their love for each other, to enjoy each other, to know each other. Mary, the perpetual virgin, never menstruating, never reaching to her husband in love, is as unreal to me as the pictures of an emasculated Jesus who could not have lifted a hammer or a saw.[2]

We agree. If marriage is God's sacred gift to us, it can be so for all who engage in it—for Mary as well as for the rest of us. We who are married can receive the gift with gratitude and strive to make marriage what it is meant to be.

MARRIAGE IS A METAPHOR FOR GOD'S RELATIONSHIP WITH US

Not only is marriage a gift from God, but also it serves as a metaphor for God's relationship with us. The first mention of marriage in scripture states that a husband "clings" to his wife (Gen. 2:24). The verb *clings* is also used to describe the Hebrews' relationship with God. Thus, Moses exhorted Israel: "You shall fear the Lord your God; him alone you shall worship; to him you shall hold fast, and by his name you shall swear" (Deut. 10:20). "Hold fast" is the same verb translated "clings" in Genesis. You can understand something of what it means to hold fast to God by reflecting on how you cling to your mate.

Jeremiah often used marital imagery in proclaiming God's message. He compared a failing marriage with a degenerating relationship between the people and God:

> If a man divorces his wife and she goes from him and
>   becomes another man's wife, will he return to her?
> Would not such a land be greatly polluted?
> You have played the whore with many lovers;
>   and would you return to me? says the LORD.
>
> (Jeremiah 3:1)

Through the prophet God said to Israel, "Your current relationship to me is like that of a wife who has been unfaithful to her husband." In both cases, unfaithfulness wounds the relationship.

In various other places, Jeremiah phrased the relationship between God and Israel using marital imagery. For instance, God called Israel "my beloved" (Jer. 11:15). And scripture calls God the "husband" of Israel (Jer. 31:32).

The New Testament compares the relationship between Christ and his church to that of husband and wife:

> Husbands, love your wives, just as Christ loved the church
> and gave himself up for her, in order to make her holy by
> cleansing her with the washing of water by the word, so as to

present the church to himself in splendor, without a spot or wrinkle or anything of the kind—yes, so that she may be holy and without blemish. In the same way, husbands should love their wives as they do their own bodies. He who loves his wife loves himself. . . . "For this reason a man will leave his father and mother and be joined to his wife, and the two will become one flesh." This is a great mystery, and I am applying it to Christ and the church. (Ephesians 5:25-32)

The occurrence of such metaphors in scripture suggests that we can learn something about each relationship from the other. Reflecting on our relationship with God can teach us how to build a better marriage. Reflecting on the nature of marriage can teach us how to develop a more meaningful faith.

MARRIAGE IS A SPIRITUAL TRAINING GROUND

As we noted earlier, some people believe that a celibate life provides a greater capacity for godliness than a married life. But we agree with Thomas Merton that marriage is a vocation: "The ordinary way to holiness and to the fullness of Christian life is marriage. Most men and women will become saints in the married state."[3] Instead of deflecting spiritual growth, marriage can be a nurturing context in which spiritual growth takes place. Marriage provides an ideal setting for learning and practicing Christian virtues, for growing in grace and knowledge of Jesus Christ, and for giving and receiving spiritual guidance.

Unfortunately, while many couples use their faith to provide a more stable ground for their marriage, fewer use their marriage as a school for Christian growth. They may attend church regularly and make a wholehearted effort to live out their faith daily, but they do not share spiritual concerns with each other. They do not encourage each other's spiritual quest or discuss their faith with each other.

Why not? In some cases, embarrassment deters them. As one man put it:

> Maybe it sounds silly, but I've always found it hard to talk about spiritual things with my wife—even though we go to church regularly. I think it's because she knows me so well, and I don't want to sound more religious than I really am. I mean, what if I started talking to her about my faith and then she said something like, "Oh yeah, if you're so religious, how come you hollered at me the other day?" I don't want her to think that I'm getting holier-than-thou with her.

This man's concern is understandable. Some people use religious jargon to verbally whip a spouse into submission. And some people mouth pious phrases but do not practice what they preach. If you want your marriage to function as a spiritual training ground, you must break through the wall of embarrassment so that you can openly and freely discuss spiritual matters.

You can create a more open atmosphere for such discussion by agreeing to the following four premises:

1. We yearn to grow spiritually and to strengthen our marriage. That requires us to discuss spiritual matters.

2. We will refrain from using "faith talk" to gain advantage or to win an argument.

3. We will honestly tell each other if we feel that the other person violates the second premise at any time.

4. Neither of us will allow any such violations to deter us from continuing to discuss spiritual matters. We will forgive violations and view them as lessons learned.

Another reason for the failure to discuss spiritual matters is a feeling of inadequacy. We've often heard such statements as: "I'm not a theologian"; "I haven't had much religious training since I was a kid in Sunday school." Again, we understand that you might feel hesitant to discuss spiritual matters with your spouse if you're not sure you can use the appropriate words or put your thoughts into the proper spiritual language. But keep these points in mind:

- *Your manner of phrasing—whether in prayer or in discussion with your spouse—matters little to God.* After all, God knows your thoughts anyway: "Even before a word is on my tongue, O Lord, you know it completely" (Ps. 139:4). The inadequacy of your language does not disappoint or offend God. Making the effort and saying something poorly are better than saying nothing at all. Think of it this way: You would prefer that your spouse expressed love to you in fumbling words rather than saying nothing. In the same way, God wants you to articulate your concerns regardless of how inadequate you feel your words are.

- *All of us are inadequate.* Trying to discern and express the ways of God certainly leads each of us to the point where we admit, "Such knowledge is too wonderful for me; it is so high that I cannot attain it" (Ps. 139:6). A pastor expressed this truth when he said: "From time to time I have thought about preaching on the glory of God. But so far I don't feel that I can put together the words that would do justice to God's glory."

- *The purpose of discussing spiritual matters is not to demonstrate spiritual acumen but to grow and become more adept.* In matters of spiritual growth, you need to express your ideas rather than impress your mate. Efforts at expression open doors to new understanding and growth; efforts at impression lead only to dead ends.

One other deterrent is that many couples simply do not realize the possibilities for spiritual growth that marriage affords. What a joyous discovery it is when spouses realize that they can turn to each other and establish a spiritual training ground for themselves! When we lead marriage enrichment seminars, we encourage couples to explore the spiritual potential of their relationship. One couple asked us for help. "We want to go on a retreat," they told us, "just the two of us. What materials can you recommend for us to use?" They welcomed our suggestions and planned a weekend together. And the outcome was precisely what they had hoped—a more vibrant marriage and a more meaningful faith.

We recommend such retreats. However, they are only a more intensive way to do what you can do in some measure every day. You can nurture each other spiritually not only in set-aside times but also in the routine of day-to-day living. As Kathleen Norris has observed, the true mystics "are not those who contemplate holiness in isolation, reaching godlike illumination in serene silence, but those who manage to find God in a life filled with noise, the demands of other people and relentless daily duties that can consume the self."[4]

FACE-TO-FACE

Begin by working separately. Complete each of the following statements about your spouse. Write your responses on a sheet of paper or in your couple's journal.

1. You help fulfill my intimacy needs when you . . .

2. You strengthen me emotionally because you . . .

3. I feel better able to handle life's challenges and stresses because you . . .

4. Some experiences we have shared that I found especially meaningful are . . .

5. You help me feel closer to God because you . . .

Talk about your responses. How many of them are similar? What surprised you about your spouse's responses? What positive experiences can you bring more frequently into your marriage? What other experiences could you add that would achieve similar results? For instance, what could your spouse do or say that would make you feel closer to God?

Pray together, thanking God for the many ways you have enriched each other.

PRAY TOGETHER

Loving God, we thank you for bringing us together in your gift of marriage. We thank you for the ways we have enriched each other and have grown in our faith. Continue to nurture us so that we may likewise nurture each other and deepen our intimacy with each other and with you. In Jesus' name we pray. Amen.

PART I

IN A SAFE PLACE

I am secure in my marriage.
I know that I can be myself
and my husband will still love me.
This security has allowed me to grow
as an individual and as a wife.

—Beth, a wife of twenty-six years

2

A Secure Place to Share

I call upon you, for you will answer me, O God;
    incline your ear to me, hear my words.
Wondrously show your steadfast love,
O Savior of those who seek refuge from their
    adversaries at your right hand.
Guard me as the apple of the eye; hide me
    in the shadow of your wings.

—Psalm 17:6-8

We were walking in the park on a sunny day with our young granddaughter, Krista. She kept hopping from one spot to another. "I have to walk in the shade every ten steps," she explained, "or I'll die." We assured her that we didn't want anything to happen to her and slowed our pace so she could count her steps and jump into a patch of shade every tenth step. But then we came to an area with no shade in sight.

"What are you going to do now?" we asked.

She surveyed the situation, then calmly placed herself so she could step into our shadows. "I'll be safe there," she told us.

Krista found safety in our shadows. The psalmist found safety in the shadow of God's wings. We all need a place of safety—a place where we feel secure from assaults on our well-being and where we feel secure talking about the thoughts and feelings swirling inside us.

YOU NEED TO SHARE

Being able to talk about your inner life is essential to your emotional and physical health. God calls you to help others by being a burden-bearer: "Bear one another's burdens, and in this way you will fulfill the law of Christ" (Gal. 6:2). Implicit in this command, however, is the call to be a burden-sharer as well. If others need you to help bear their burdens, you also need them to help bear yours. You need to share your triumphs and joys as well as your failures and frustrations.

If you're like us, you probably don't have a problem talking about your joys and successes. But what about the underside of your life—your anxieties, fears, doubts, failures, and struggles? Your emotional and physical well-being depend on your being able to share them. David discovered this truth when he bottled up his guilt about sin: "While I kept silence, my body wasted away through my groaning all day long" (Ps. 32:3).

Similarly, we have known people to suffer various afflictions as they struggled silently with a problem instead of sharing it with a spouse or friend. "I don't want to impose my work problems on my wife," Greg explained. Greg has a stressful managerial position in a high-tech company. He views his work problems as personal challenges: "I can deal with them myself. I don't have to involve Patty."

It may sound as if Greg is being loving and courageous. Yet silence in the face of inner turmoil does not indicate strength; it is an act of self-destruction. Not surprisingly, Greg's efforts at silent coping took a toll on his physical and mental health.

In addition to the personal benefits for your emotional and physical health, talking about your inner life is essential to the well-being of your relationship with God and with the important people in your life. David experienced a joyous liberation and a restoration of his intimacy with God after he confessed his sin: "Then I acknowledged my sin to you, / and I did not hide my iniquity; / I said, 'I will confess my transgressions to the LORD,' / and you forgave the guilt of my sin" (Ps. 32:5).

Patty let Greg know that his reluctance to tell her about his problems at work, no matter how loving his motivations, was unacceptable. She told him:

> I want you to tell me about what's going on at work. I *need* you to tell me. Otherwise, I don't know what to make of it when I see you looking so glum. Usually I decide it's because of something I've done. Besides, I want to support you, and I can't do that if you shut me out.

Greg and Patty made these statements in the course of discussing their frayed marital intimacy with us. It was clear to us and to Patty that Greg needed to share his struggles with her in order to restore their feelings of intimacy. Eventually, this need became apparent to Greg as well.

Sharing increases intimacy because it avoids what we call self-compression—withholding yourself to the point that few, if any, people know much about you. Carried to the extreme, self-compression can cause an individual to become virtually nonexistent to others. And as the pioneer psychologist William James wrote in the 1890s, "no more fiendish punishment" can be conceived of for a person than to be in society and yet be treated as nonexistent:

> If no one turned round when we entered, answered when we spoke, or minded what we did, but if every person we met "cut us dead," and acted as if we were non-existing things, a kind of rage and impotent despair would ere long well up in us, from which the cruellest bodily tortures would be a relief; for these would make us feel that, however bad might be our plight, we had not sunk to such a depth as to be unworthy of attention at all.[1]

"Unworthy of attention" is a biting phrase. Yet how can anyone attend to your concerns if you never reveal them? How can anyone bear your burdens if you keep them closeted within you? Indeed, how can anyone relate to you as a close friend if you withhold information that reveals who you are? Early in our discussion with Patty and Greg, Patty made a telling comment about their relationship:

> I've known him for ten years. But there are times when I feel like I don't really know him at all. I don't know what's going on with him. It's like I'm playing a guessing game where I'm trying to figure out what he's thinking or feeling or what's bothering him. To be honest, I don't want to live with a stranger any more.

You can't feel intimate with someone who is a mystery to you. You have to know something of what he or she believes, feels, and desires. And your spouse needs to know the same about you. Not everything, of course. No one ever fully knows another person. Yet without some knowledge, intimacy with God and others is impossible.

That is why Jesus' response to Philip's request to "show us the Father" is crucial: "Whoever has seen me has seen the Father" (John 14:8-9). In essence, Jesus was saying: "Philip, in me you have a living portrait of God. Look at the way I relate to people. Listen to the things I teach you. Watch how I show my concern for you. And in these things, you know something about the Father."

In summary, marriage partners need to talk about their inner lives for the sake of each one's well-being. So why do many people find self-revelation difficult? It's because most people realize—consciously or subconsciously—that sharing makes a person vulnerable to devaluation.

You Need to Be Secure from Devaluation

No matter what we tell God, we do not have to worry that God will value us any less than before our revelation. Throughout the scriptures, the message is the same: Turn to God, confess your sins, and you will receive forgiveness and restoration. When David confessed his sin, he encountered no shock, no disgust, no rejection from God. He found the forgiveness that restored his well-being. "If we confess our sins, he who is faithful and just will forgive us our sins and cleanse us from all unrighteousness" (1 John 1:9).

But what about sharing with other people? What if you express spiritual doubts to a friend, only to have your shocked friend lecture you about the wrongness of such thoughts? What if you admit to your spouse that you feel anxious and fearful, only to have him or her say, "I thought you had more courage than that"? Or what if the dark things you share with your spouse cause him or her to lose respect or even love for you?

When John Powell was writing his book *Why Am I Afraid to Tell You Who I Am?* he mentioned the title to an acquaintance. The acquaintance asked if Powell wanted to know his answer to the question. When Powell replied affirmatively, the person said, "I am afraid to tell you who I am, because if I tell you who I am, you may not like who I am, and it's all that I have."[2]

No wonder you might hesitate to bare your inner being. Unquestionably, sharing makes you vulnerable to reproof, disappointment, disdain, and ridicule. However, having a secure place to share—a personal confessional where you encounter understanding and help—encourages personal growth and intimacy.

Marriage can provide this place of security, but such security doesn't happen automatically. Responding to each other with sensitivity and understanding does not come naturally. It requires patience and practice. Moreover, security can be breached in subtle ways. We discovered an example in our discussion with Greg and Patty. Greg based his reluctance to share partly on earlier experiences he had had with Patty:

> One thing I've always wanted to do is to get out of this company and start my own business. But years ago when I brought up the subject, Patty cut me off before I even finished telling her my ideas. She said it was too risky. She said she liked having a stable income. So I never mentioned the idea again.

We rebuke our partner for sharing openly with us in many subtle ways. One way is to interrupt or cut off our mate before he or she finishes talking. Patty's rejection of Greg's idea before she had heard his full explanation is an example. She was so anxious to express her feelings that she missed an opportunity for him to share his aspirations.

"You shouldn't . . ." is another common rebuke. "I feel guilty about turning down that committee at church," a woman says to her husband. "You shouldn't feel guilty," he responds brusquely. Now she feels guilty about feeling guilty and dissatisfied with her effort to share with her husband. The bonds of intimacy have loosened a bit at this moment.

Still another way we rebuke is to trivialize a concern of our partner. "I hope my health isn't deteriorating," a man says to his wife after his annual checkup reveals arthritis in some of his joints. "That's nothing. Everyone your age has the same problem. Be thankful it's nothing worse," she replies. Her response doesn't ease his concerns. He decides not to tell her that he's also worried that he doesn't have as much stamina as he used to.

Analyzing our spouse's motives is another form of rebuke. Greg did this to Patty. She said it was the final straw that brought them to us:

> I couldn't handle it anymore. If I tried to get him to talk about what was going on at work, he'd say that I didn't really want to know. That I wasn't really interested in it. That I was just trying to satisfy my female curiosity. If I asked what was bothering him, he'd say that it wasn't about us and that I was asking because I was insecure. And when I told him I had thought about leaving him, he said I was trying to hurt him because I was mad that he didn't talk more.

Notice that every time Patty raised a concern, Greg turned it against her by demeaning her motives.

People who use the various forms of rebuke we have described may not think of their responses as forms of devaluation: "I simply expressed my opinion, just as he (she) expressed his (hers)." They may not be aware of the effect that those "opinions" have on the partner: "I didn't mean for her (him) to stop talking to me about the matter."

That is why we say that establishing a secure place for sharing requires patience and practice. Later, we'll discuss specific ways to establish your secure place. First, let's explore further the meaning of security.

Security Means Acceptance

Recall what the acquaintance said to John Powell: "I am afraid to tell you who I am, because if I tell you who I am, you may not like who I am, and it's all that I have." You feel secure only when you sense that someone accepts you for who you are.

God accepts you for who you are. In the words of the old hymn, we come to God "just as I am, without one plea."

God's acceptance provides the pattern for human acceptance—and God's pattern often differs from ours. For many of us, acceptance means approval: "I want you to accept me as I am, to approve of the kind of person I am." For others, acceptance means there is no need to change: "I want you to accept me as I am and allow me to continue to be what I am." But God's acceptance of us as we are does not mean that God approves of our behavior or wants us to continue in the same way. Rather, God accepts us as we are in order to begin the work of molding us into the likeness of Jesus Christ.

Similarly, in marriage your partner doesn't have to approve of all you do or of your continuing to do it in order to provide a secure place for you to share. On the contrary, an important benefit of sharing with your spouse is gaining his or her help in becoming the person God has created you to be.

Jack struggled with lustful thoughts for most of his seven-year marriage to Suzie. He supervised many attractive young women in his office and found himself thinking about them when he returned home. Eventually, he had a brief affair with one of them. Overcome with guilt and remorse, he confessed the affair to Suzie. He also confessed that even though the affair deeply shamed him, he still struggled with lustful thoughts.

Fortunately, Jack had a secure place in which to share. He knew that his betrayal would deeply hurt Suzie, which heightened his agony over telling her. Yet he was sure that she would not reject or leave him:

> For a time after I told her, I thought she might divorce me. It was even more painful for her than I thought it would be. I couldn't say that I would've blamed her if she had kicked me out. But she didn't. She forgave me and is helping me deal with my problem. I keep a picture of Suzie on my desk. And whenever I start feeling lust for one of the women in my office, I go look at that picture. Or I give her a call and tell her I love her. And she calls me every day to remind me that she loves me. It really helps. I can honestly say that the problem is much less now. Even the thought of betraying her again makes me ill.

Suzie accepted Jack, but she did not approve of his behavior and would not allow it to continue. Her acceptance did not mean: "What you are doing is okay." It did not mean: "I won't expect you to change." Rather, it meant: "I understand who you are. I forgive you for hurting me. I will stand by you and help you in your struggles."

An explanation is needed here to prevent misinterpretation. We do not want to imply that you should try to change everything you find bothersome in your mate. Every marriage involves two people who love, cherish, and annoy each other in a number of ways. You are married to a flawed individual. So is your spouse. We like the piece of wisdom a young woman who had been married for two years shared with us:

> It didn't take long for me to realize the ways he annoys me. Like throwing his clothes on the chair instead of hanging them up. And not taking the trash out until I remind him about it. It was when he complained about my always squeezing the toothpaste tube from the top that it hit me: I also annoy him! This was a turning point for me. I decided that we each owe the other at least two or three annoyances. We can live with them.

For some situations, acceptance means learning to live with the annoyance, knowing that your spouse is doing the same for you. For other situations, acceptance means maintaining your commitment to each other while working together to change the behavior. Security provides the context for doing both. Ongoing prayer for guidance provides wisdom for discerning conditions you can live with and conditions that must change.

Security Means an Honest Relationship

The psalmist declared, "Break the arm of the wicked and evil-doers" (Ps. 10:15). On more than one occasion the psalmist literally called on God to engage in battering the people the psalmist defined as evil. If you find such statements appalling in light of Jesus' command to love our enemies, you can still admire the psalmist for feeling so secure with God that he could pour out even his most vicious thoughts.

The psalmist had an honest relationship with God, a relationship of openness and integrity. He did not pretend with God to be something he was not. And for the psalmist that was the start of becoming what God wanted him to be. The same is true for each of us. Our growth toward godliness begins with recognizing and acknowledging our ungodliness.

In brief, honesty before God is the necessary prelude to spiritual growth. As Jesus pointed out, the tax collector who honestly admitted his sins to God was justified, rather than the Pharisee who presented himself as someone who practiced righteousness (Luke 18:9-14). The tax collector understood something that the Pharisee did not: God gives us the security to be open about our failings, to be free of the need to impress others or to justify ourselves, to be honest about our desires and our concerns.

Similarly, honesty lies at the heart of a healthy marital relationship. Security in your love and mutual trust frees you to be, to feel, to express, to explore, to become. You can discuss matters with each other that you cannot talk about with others because you know your spouse will not rebuke or reject you.

Kevin and his wife, Sally, told us of their experience in an adult Sunday school class. The teacher frequently made a point that Kevin questioned. Whenever he tried to explore the matter, however, the teacher quickly informed Kevin of the "orthodox" position, which permitted no questions or doubts. Although the teacher's statement of orthodoxy did not end Kevin's doubts, it unfortunately ended his raising questions in class:

> I was beginning to feel like a troublemaker. So now I just sit and listen. When we get home, Sally and I can talk about the things that were said. She can't answer all my questions, but at least she's willing to listen and explore them with me. And that really helps.

Kevin and Sally are committed Christians who help each other grow in their faith. Where a Sunday school teacher failed, an honest marital relationship succeeded in providing a secure place for Kevin to grapple with his uncertainties and to develop as a Christian.

Again, an explanation is needed. Honesty in your relationship with your spouse does not mean that you say anything you please whenever you wish or however you choose to say it. God calls you to speak the truth "in love" (Eph. 4:15) and to "bridle" your tongue (James 1:26). In other words, you need some checkpoint between your brain and tongue. Every thought that pops into your mind should not jump out of your mouth.

Rather, your words should be "useful for building up," and they should "give grace to those who hear" (Eph. 4:29).

Honesty does not mean insensitivity or bluntness. The challenge of faith is to enjoy the freedom of an honest relationship in the context of loving concern for your partner. If you feel the need to share something with your spouse but are uncertain about whether it would be wise to tell him or her, ask yourself the following questions:[3]

1. *Why do I want to share this?* You may be tempted to confess something to your spouse to relieve guilt, even though you know your confession will hurt your spouse. Confessing to God or to a pastor or counselor before you decide whether to tell your spouse may be wise.

Or you may be tempted to say something hurtful at a time when you are tired or frustrated. These words may seem to express your honest feelings at the moment but really are a product of your present mood. When the mood passes, the words will be meaningless. So they are better left unsaid.

2. *Who will benefit?* Whenever you share feelings and thoughts with your spouse, potential benefits exist. Through sharing you may rid yourself of a load of guilt. Obviously you gain from this sharing, but what if sharing merely transfers your guilt to your spouse? Neither your spouse nor your marriage will benefit. The goal of sharing is to build up each partner and to nurture your marriage in the process. So when you share with each other, consider who benefits.

3. *With whom should I share this?* Although you probably can share more thoughts with your spouse than with anyone else, at times someone else may be a more appropriate listener. For example, when a husband confessed to his pregnant wife that he didn't feel ready for parenthood and was uncertain of whether he could love their child, he subjected her to unnecessary stress. Fortunately, his doubts vanished when he held his newborn son for the first time. But he would have saved his wife much agony by confessing his uncertainties to a trusted friend or relative.

4. *Will this sharing make us feel closer to each other?* The answer has both short-term and long-term considerations. Sharing that your spouse annoys you in some way most likely won't immediately make you feel closer to each other. But in the long run, it could have this result. And the long run is what's most important. In a premarital counseling session, a bride-to-be shared with the counselor and her future husband that his tendency to criticize her family bothered her. He acknowledged that he often harped on the faults of her family, but her comment obviously hurt him. With the help of the counselor, he came to understand the reason for his harsh judgments and learned to control his words. In the long run, everyone benefited.

Marital Security Is Built, Not Given

With God, security is a given: "Everything that the Father gives me will come to me, and anyone who comes to me I will never drive away" (John 6:37). You may come to God in prayer and not receive what you desire. You may not even receive what you think you need. Yet you will always receive something of what God knows you need. You will never go away empty-handed.

Christian author Ken Gire tells of his time in the wilderness "of pain, of humiliation, of uncertainty, of loneliness and desperation" after he answered what he thought was God's call to write.[4] For a number of years, he sold nothing. Financially and emotionally, he reached the point of desperation. None of his cries to God for help seemed to bear fruit. Finally, he secured a writing job. In retrospect, he could see that his time in the wilderness had prepared him for his calling, and all the frustration and suffering were necessary experiences for him to become the writer he wanted and prayed to be. Gire wrote,

> How could I know the feelings of the desperate if I had not been desperate myself? How could I know the feelings of the poor if I had not been poor myself? How could I know the feelings of the confused if I had not been confused myself? Or depressed myself? Or abandoned?[5]

In retrospect he saw that time of struggle as an answer to his prayer to be an effective writer. He could see that he had been secure in the hands of God all along.

Security with your spouse, on the other hand, is not a given. It must be built. How? Think about the nature of your security with God. God always listens to what you say, meeting you not with devaluation but with help and support. Accordingly, if you want to build security in your marriage, you need to genuinely listen to your spouse, abstain from demeaning remarks when your spouse tells you something, maintain confidentiality, and express appreciation for your spouse's openness with you. Let's look at each of these qualities.

Really Listen to Your Spouse

When your spouse wants to share a concern, you need to genuinely listen. Don't fall prey to pretend listening, where you nod but inwardly are disinterested and only partly attentive. Concentrate on your partner's words and expressions, and become absorbed with his or her concerns. Engaged listening requires energy. However, this energy is well spent because listening will help your spouse feel more secure. Listening communicates that you care, understand, and support your mate.

Distractions are enemies of engaged listening, so you will have to resist them. The tendency to respond before your partner has had a chance to finish a thought is another enemy; you will need to curb your urge to interrupt. And particularly for men, the tendency to offer a quick solution is an enemy. More often than not, your spouse needs to talk, not get a quick fix from you. Matt told us how he learned this lesson:

When Shelley came home frustrated by a problem at work, I would listen for a few minutes, then tell her what she ought to do. This only made her angry and more frustrated. I realized that my quick answers were a put-down of sorts, suggesting that I could easily handle problems that she couldn't. Now I listen until she is finished. Then I just ask her, "What can I do to help you?" Usually, she tells me just to listen. I only give her my opinion or advice if she asks for it.

Shelley says that now Matt is a great help to her as she copes with stressful work situations. His engaged listening gives her a secure place to share her concerns.

Abstain from Devaluation

We make this point again because it is so easy to fall prey to subtle forms of devaluation. Matt thought he was being helpful when he offered Shelley solutions to her work problems. Only when she screamed at him one day, "I don't want you to solve it; I just want you to listen," did he realize that he had been sending her a subtle message that she was incompetent to deal with problems.

A common form of subtle devaluation is responding with quick solutions. "You shouldn't . . . ," as we noted earlier, is another. Another time Shelley was the one who put down Matt when he told her that he was worried about a colleague's problems dealing with clients. "You shouldn't worry about that," Shelley broke in. "You're not responsible for his behavior." She wanted to ease his worry, but her statement had a different effect. "Don't tell me how I should feel," he said hotly. Shelley realized her mistake and encouraged Matt to talk about his concern.

We hope that these examples illustrate why security is not a given but must be built—even in marriage. As a way of helping you break the habit of demeaning responses, we suggest that you and your spouse agree to the following covenant:

- I will share myself with you so that you don't have to guess what I am thinking or feeling and so that we may grow ever closer to each other.

- I will strive to listen without demeaning you in any way so that you can freely share yourself with me.

- Speaking the truth in love, I will tell you when you respond to me in a way that inhibits my sharing. I will assume that such responses from you are unintentional.

- I ask you to work with me so that my responses encourage you to share yourself with me.

Maintain Confidentiality

"The Bible says to confess your sins to one another," we heard a Sunday school teacher say. "The trick is to find someone who won't confess them, in turn, to others." Without the assurance of confidentiality, a relationship is insecure, and spouses will not share important information about themselves with each other.

But surely, confidentiality is not an issue in marriage! Or is it? Actually, we have frequently observed breaches of confidentiality in our work with couples' groups—often unintentional but breaches nonetheless. We have heard one spouse say something about the other that obviously embarrassed the other person. In informal gatherings, we have heard offhand comments that were unsettling, such as the woman who mentioned that her husband (standing beside her) worried too much about their finances. As a Christian, he had the uneasy feeling that his worries might indicate a weak faith. Didn't Jesus say not to fret about such matters? He was horrified when she blithely revealed to the group his habit of fretting, and he vowed not to share money concerns with her in the future.

In Ephesians 4:29 Paul offered an admonition that can serve as a basic method for maintaining confidentiality: "Let no evil talk come out of your mouths, but only what is useful for building up." Conversations with others are times to share positive comments about your spouse, not occasions for recruiting a group to help you deal with irksome habits. The woman who spoke of her husband's worrying may have wanted others to agree that he worried too much and desired their help in encouraging him to change. If that was her intent, she chose the wrong way to remedy the situation.

EXPRESS APPRECIATION FOR THE DISCLOSURE

In a place where you are punished, you feel no security. You feel secure in places where you find affirmation. A demeaning response is a form of punishment. The expression of appreciation is an affirmation. You build security by letting your spouse know that you appreciate his or her disclosure of feelings.

Sometimes the appreciation can be verbal: "Thanks for letting me know how you feel," or "I'm glad you told me about your anxiety because I've been concerned too." Appreciation can also be nonverbal—a hug, a kiss, a smile.

Expressing appreciation along with engaged listening, refraining from devaluation, and maintaining confidentiality sends your spouse a message—a vastly different message from the one John Powell's acquaintance gave him. Your message says, "I am happy to tell you who I am, because, when I tell you, you listen to me, you accept me, you help me, and that's all I need. You are a place of security."

FACE-TO-FACE

Read Psalm 40 together. Reread it verse by verse; then answer the following questions in your couple's journal:

1. What feelings did the psalmist freely share with God?

2. What did God do that made the psalmist feel secure in his sharing?

3. In what ways can you use your answers to the second question to maintain or enhance your marriage as a place of security?

Based on your answers to the third question, make specific plans for building greater security in your marriage. You might mention something your partner said or did in the past that made you feel more secure in your relationship and discuss how you can incorporate more of these experiences into everyday life. Or consider whether one or both of you need to hone your listening skills. How can you do this? Note the plans in your couple's journal.

Close with a time of prayer. Thank God for the security you have with each other, and ask God to help make your marriage an even more secure place for each of you.

PRAY TOGETHER

You are our Rock, O God. In the security of your grace, we can openly share with you all our struggles, doubts, fears, and hopes. We need to share with you. We also need to share with each other. Help us to be a secure place for each other so that we may feel as safe and be as open with each other as we are with you. Through Christ our Savior we pray. Amen.

A Protected Niche for Authenticity

O Lord, you have searched me and known me.
You know when I sit down and when I rise up;
   you discern my thoughts from far away.
You search out my path and my lying down,
   and are acquainted with all my ways.

—Psalm 139:1-3

Popular jargon today puts a premium on authenticity. He's "the real thing." She's "the genuine article." With him, "what you see is what you get." People who make such observations are saying two things: (1) That person really is what he or she appears to be, and (2) Authenticity is a highly commendable quality.

We agree that authenticity deserves praise. It provides the soil in which both faith and relationships grow and flourish. We also believe that the effort to be authentic is a lifelong pursuit. What you define as the "real thing" or the "real you" changes as you grow, mature, and gain new understanding. A distinction exists between authenticity and the authentic self. The authentic self is the self that God intends for you. Authenticity means to be what you are at each phase of your journey toward that authentic self.

God calls you to relate to others in love just as Christ did. At any stage of your growth toward your authentic self, you will fall short of this love, but you are closer to it than you were before. To be authentic is to recognize and practice the level of love you have reached without pretending to be either more or less loving than you are. To pursue your authentic self is to go beyond where you are now and to achieve new levels of love.

Being authentic is not easy. You and your spouse can help each other in the effort. When you do, you will discover that practicing authenticity nourishes your lives and your marriage.

GOD'S CALL TO AUTHENTICITY

In essence, authenticity means openness and honesty with yourself and others about who you are. Your understanding of who you are is limited and changes as you grow. Authentic persons act in agreement with their understanding of who they are.

They shun pretense, artificiality, and imitation. Striving for authenticity helps you become what God wants you to be and helps shape your marriage to agree with God's calling.

Authentic People of the Bible

Examples of people who heeded God's call to authenticity fill the Hebrew scriptures. Abraham honestly revealed his feelings when he scoffed at God's promise to give him an heir. Moses showed clarity about who he thought he was when he resisted God's call to lead the Israelites out of Egypt. He said to God, "O my LORD, I have never been eloquent. . . . I am slow of speech and slow of tongue" (Exod. 4:10). David committed adultery with Bathsheba and then had her husband killed in an effort to hide the affair. When the prophet Nathan confronted him about his deeds, David didn't try to justify them but acknowledged who he was and what he had done: "I know my transgressions, and my sin is ever before me. . . . Indeed, I was born guilty, a sinner when my mother conceived me" (Ps. 51:3, 5). Although Jeremiah answered God's call to prophesy, he complained and argued with God incessantly.

Authentic characters abound in the New Testament also. John the Baptist, clothed in camel's hair and subsisting on a diet of locusts and wild honey, demonstrated boldness in proclaiming Jesus as the awaited Messiah. John also reflected authenticity later when he experienced doubts. Instead of pretending to be certain about his earlier declaration, he told his followers to go to Jesus and ask him, "Are you the one who is to come, or are we to wait for another?" (Luke 7:20).

Look at the Twelve. With the exception of Judas, all of them seemed to be "the real thing" with their wavering faith and loyalty, their angry outbursts and jealousies.

The apostle Paul acknowledged who he was—shortcomings and all: "I find it to be a law that when I want to do what is good, evil lies close at hand" (Rom. 7:21). Overshadowing all of these persons was Jesus, who knew exactly who he was and acted accordingly. His authenticity rings true in his long discourse with the scribes and the Pharisees, recorded in John 8. In this encounter with the Jewish leaders of his day, he clearly told them who he was and why he had come. Then Jesus concluded his discourse with the astonishing disclosure: "Very truly, I tell you, before Abraham was, I am" (John 8:58).

Not only was Jesus who he said he was, but he also reserved his strongest condemnation for those who pretended to be something more than they were—the scribes and Pharisees who did "not practice what they teach" (Matt. 23:3). Jesus called them hypocrites. The Greeks used this word to refer to actors on the stage, who wore masks and pretended to be someone else. So the word *hypocrite* came to mean someone who engages in pretense and deception. A hypocrite rejects God's call to authenticity.

Pretending to be someone other than who we are is pointless. God knows who we are. As the psalmist reminded us, God has searched us and known us, even knowing the words we will speak before they reach our tongues (Ps. 139:1-4).

Authenticity Is Imperative, Not Optional

Authenticity is imperative for your relationship with God and with your mate. Both relationships require commitment. They demand that you give yourself to the other. But unless you strive to be authentic, what you give is a fabrication rather than your true self. In relationships such fabrications inevitably lead to rupture.

We have known many marriages to struggle because the commitment involved an inauthentic self of one partner. One discouraged wife told us, "After we were married, I realized I didn't know him at all." And a distraught husband of three years complained, "She changed drastically after we were married and became a different person." In each case, these marriages were floundering because the spouses felt deceived.

Committing a fabricated self to a relationship is not always a deliberate, conscious act of deception. Often individuals are unaware of who they really are. Even if they have a pretty good idea, the rite of dating and courtship seems to discourage revealing all. When you are dating, you want to make the best impression, hide any flaws, and generally be what the other person wants you to be. This doesn't allow much room for authenticity. No wonder some newlyweds begin to question after the honeymoon, "Who is this person I married?"

Jan began asking this question shortly after her marriage to Bill. A pharmaceutical salesman, Bill regularly called on the doctors in the offices where Jan worked as a receptionist. Bill's sense of humor immediately appealed to her. "He cracked me up every time he came in," she told us. Romance blossomed between the two, and within a year they married. Yet by their first anniversary, the marriage was in trouble. Jan was angry and unhappy. "Bill never takes anything seriously," she complained. "If I try to talk to him about important things like buying a house or having children, all I get are his silly wisecracks."

Bill had learned to rely on humor to sell both his products and himself to other people. Humor had brought Jan into his life, and he relied on it to keep her there. He thought that if he kept the funny lines coming, his marriage would be secure. The more troubled his marriage became, the more Bill tried to laugh away the problems. He treated humor as a magic potion that would keep his marriage healthy. It didn't work.

Bill failed to realize that he was using humor to avoid addressing issues. He turned most serious discussions into a joke. In their first significant discussion about having a baby, Bill performed a stand-up comic routine about a pregnant Jan. She told us, "He stuffed a pillow under his shirt and waddled around the room. He really was funny, and I admit that he made me laugh. But that's the way it goes every time I bring up an issue—Bill turns the discussion into a joke. The difference now is that I usually end up in tears."

Bill admitted that the idea of having children frightened

him. "It seems like such a grown-up thing to do," he told us jokingly. "I'm just not sure I'm ready to become a father with a mortgage." Fearful of the responsibilities, he tried to joke his way out of serious discussions.

Only when Bill stopped the pretense and acknowledged his overwhelming fear of responsibilities did his marriage get back on track. As Bill and Jan found out, lack of awareness is no excuse to remain inauthentic. Heeding God's call to authenticity is an imperative in developing a stable, vital relationship.

AUTHENTICITY AS KNOWING YOURSELF

"I wonder if I've been changed in the night?" asked Alice as she reflected on her situation in Wonderland. ". . . Was I the same when I got up this morning? I almost think I can remember feeling a little different. But if I'm not the same, the next question is 'Who in the world am I?' Ah, *that's* the great puzzle!"[1]

You don't have to be in Wonderland to know that Alice's last question reflects the universal human struggle. At times we all find ourselves puzzled about who we are. Knowing ourselves is an elusive and difficult task; we need the assistance of others. Sometimes a friend, relative, or pastor can help. Often a spouse is in the best position to assist with this task. The process of self-discovery may uncover an unsettling characteristic (one that bothers you) or a pleasantly surprising quality (one that makes you feel better about yourself).

Consider Tim's unsettling experience:

I've always been defensive about my mistakes. For years, my wife, Marcy, pointed out how I seemed compelled to justify all my actions. Even if I did something wrong or hurtful, I would find a reason that seemed, at least to me, to justify it. Finally I admitted that Marcy was right. It's been a struggle, but I think I've gotten to the point where I can own up when I goof. I used to feel that I would be less of a husband and less of a Christian if I messed up. Marcy has helped me to see that I don't always have to be right. Learning to acknowledge my mistakes instead of defending them has freed me and revitalized our marriage.

Although this revelation about himself initially disturbed him, Tim eventually found it liberating. "What a load off my shoulders," he told us, "when I realized I didn't have to be right about everything. This discovery has turned my life around."

Wanda had a quite different experience. She learned something about herself that pleasantly surprised her. It also turned out to be a major turning point in her life. Here's her story:

Ten years ago, I was in an unhappy marriage and out of work. I sat at home, ate all day, and got so heavy that I was ashamed to leave the house. Then a pastor in our community came to visit me. He recognized right away that my life was a mess and offered to meet regularly with me to talk about my problems. One day he said to me, "You know, you are a very intelligent person." I was shocked. I thought of myself as a dummy. I asked him why he said this, thinking maybe he was just trying to be nice. But he told me it was because of the way I thought about and analyzed things. It took a while for his words to sink in, but eventually, I believed him. And this realization changed my life. For the first time in my memory, I had the confidence to try to get out of the rut I was in. I went to Weight Watchers and lost the pounds I had put on. I learned how to drive. I got a job. I'm back in church. I feel like a new person!

Self-Knowledge Comes through Humility

Tim and Wanda had a characteristic in common: Both needed to learn humility in order to become more authentic. *Humility* may be one of the most misunderstood terms in the Christian's vocabulary. To many people, humility means belittling themselves or thinking of themselves as less competent or less worthy than others. But this is not the New Testament meaning.

Two Greek words in the New Testament can be translated "humility." One *(prautes)* means "lowly in spirit" or "meek," and the other *(tapeinophrosune)* means "lowly in mind." Neither word means "self-abasement." Rather, humility is lowly in the sense that it opposes pride. Humility means putting yourself on the same level as everyone else. It does not mean that you avoid thinking or saying anything positive about yourself.

Jesus told his disciples, "Take my yoke upon you, and learn from me; for I am gentle and humble in heart" (Matt. 11:29). In essence, he said, "I'm one of you. I understand your struggles and strivings. You can take my yoke because I know what it's like to be human." When Paul wrote to the Corinthians that he was "humble" when face-to-face with them (2 Cor. 10:1), he said, in essence, "When I was with you, I didn't act as if I was superior to you. I was one of you."

When you identify with the human condition and see yourself as neither better nor worse than others, you practice humility. You acknowledge that you are neither worthless (after all, God loved you enough to send Christ to die for you) nor flawless (all have sinned). And your self-understanding is more realistic and authentic because you recognize and acknowledge your strengths as well as your shortcomings.

Spouses Build Each Other's Self-Knowledge

"Now I know only in part" (1 Cor. 13:12), wrote the apostle Paul. Like other kinds of knowledge, self-knowledge is always "only in part." Dr. Paul Tournier describes the journey of self-knowledge as "progress from uneasiness to uneasiness," a "gradual feeling our way along a road of discovery, rather than a full and complete knowledge of ourselves."[2]

You will never reach the point of being able to identify all your strengths and shortcomings, nor can your spouse. Over time you grow in understanding yourself and your mate, and you can help build each other's self-knowledge.

Spouses can help us learn more about ourselves in three ways. The first is by using a *gentle admonition*. Like Tim's wife, Marcy, you can identify areas in which your mate needs to improve or develop skills. Admonition is a delicate task. No one wants a resident critic who constantly points a finger at his or her flaws. Yet notice how Tim was grateful to Marcy for helping him overcome his defensiveness. The idea is to help each other grow in self-understanding so that both of you grow spiritually. This type of growth is more likely to happen if you take a gentle approach. Consider these admonitions:

> "You don't have to justify what you did; we all make mistakes" (rather than, "Stop being so defensive!").

> "I know you didn't intend it, but teasing me about my forgetfulness really did hurt" (rather than, "Why were you so mean to me?").

> "It would really help me balance our accounts if you'd record the amount when you write a check" (rather than, "Your irresponsibility makes my life really difficult").

In these examples the same message—"You are too defensive"; "You misuse humor when you tease someone"; "You need to be more responsible"—is said in two ways. In our experience, the gentle approach generally succeeds more often than the harsher tack in motivating a person to change.

A second way to help each other gain self-understanding is through *affirmation*. While gentle admonition corrects the tendency to pride, affirmation corrects the tendency to abase oneself. Like Wanda, your spouse may not know or acknowledge some of his or her finest qualities. Affirmation recognizes and encourages those qualities.

Affirmation may involve pointing out a good quality that

your mate seems to overlook. For example, a husband told his wife, who considered other women in her church to be much more spiritual than she was, "You exemplify what it means to be a Christian as much as anyone I know."

Affirmation may include encouraging your mate in an area where he or she feels inadequate. A wife told her husband who questioned his abilities as a new father:

> I have no doubt that you're going to be a great father. It's only a question of time before you realize it too. You just need to become more comfortable handling the baby, and then your confidence will grow.

The third way to help each other gain self-understanding is to *model the appropriate behavior*. Counter your mate's cynicism with optimism, irresponsibility with accountability, and stinginess with generosity. A minister admitted that he learned something important about himself by watching his wife:

> You'd think that as a minister, I would be really sensitive to people's needs. But I have to confess that I often am so concerned with what people are thinking about my performance that I neglect to focus on their needs. I learned this by watching my wife. I would see her inquire about how someone was doing when I hadn't even bothered to ask. I had only been interested in the person's opinion of my sermon or handling of the building campaign. I'll admit, I wasn't all that concerned with what was happening in the person's life. But I'm trying to change. I've seen how people respond to Mary Beth's warmth and care. So I've been working on being more sensitive to people's needs and less concerned about

how I come across to them. I think I'm making progress. And that's because of her Christlike example.

Of course, sometimes a gentle admonition may also be necessary. That was true for Tim. Although Marcy did not respond in a defensive manner or try to justify her shortcomings, her modeling was not sufficient. Only repeated reminders caused him finally to recognize and change his defensive behavior.

AUTHENTICITY AS BEING YOURSELF

After the Resurrection, Jesus appeared to his disciples on several occasions. Since Thomas was not present with the others when Jesus first came to them, he didn't believe the disciples when they said they had seen the Lord. He told them, "Unless I see the mark of the nails in his hands, and put my finger in the mark of the nails and my hand in his side, I will not believe" (John 20:25).

Thomas's assertion gave rise to the expression "doubting Thomas," which is not a compliment. Thomas could just as well be called "courageous Thomas," however, for being the lone dissenter in a close-knit group takes a good deal of courage. Thomas had the strength of character to express his doubts rather than to pretend he believed something he didn't. Thomas was being himself.

To be yourself means to speak and act in accord with your understanding of who you are. It also to means to act in accord with your understanding of who God wants you to become, a topic we'll explore in the next chapter.

Being Who You Are

Our environment often pressures us to be someone other than our authentic selves and to behave in ways that go against our inclinations and our understanding of ourselves. In contrast, marriage can offer a protected niche where you can be yourself. In an honest relationship you do not have to suppress doubts or pretend to be cheerful when you feel sad or anxious. You can express anger and irritability. You don't have to appear strong and self-confident in the face of every challenge. You can admit your faults and shortcomings, ask for help, and confess that you dislike someone and struggle to exercise Christian love toward that person. You can acknowledge your good qualities and strengths without apologizing for seeming boastful.

In an authentic marriage relationship, you can relax and be yourself because your spouse accepts you and loves you for who you are. To some extent, it's like being alone with God, having the freedom to be open without apology or rationalization. However, with God, the freedom to be authentic is unconditional. With your spouse, authenticity works only within the context of some rules.

Rules for Being Yourself in Marriage

1. *Support your mate's freedom to be authentic.* To support your mate's authenticity means that you will accept a certain amount of discomfort. After all, you probably don't welcome hearing your spouse grumble, complain, or lash out in anger. Nor do you like it when your spouse seems to treat others more graciously than he or she treats you. Tricia told our marriage support group one evening: "We were at a dinner party last week, and Hal was lively and funny. We had a great time. But when we got home, he was grim and silent. It really made me mad. Why couldn't he be as vivacious with me as he was with the others?" Hal responded: "I was really zapped after work, but I didn't let on how I felt at the party."

Tricia looked surprised when we told her that Hal's behavior actually was a compliment to her and to their relationship. We explained that Hal felt free to give in to his exhaustion when he was with her, a freedom he didn't have with the others. His authenticity was a compliment to her because he trusted her to accept him in all his weariness.

2. *Honor your mate's need to understand.* Unfortunately, Hal didn't give Tricia the explanation that he later gave us. In this sense, his authenticity did not compliment her; rather, it insulted her. Tricia would have understood and felt much differently if Hal had said to her as they left the party: "I'm worn out. It was all I could do to be sociable tonight. I'm ready for some quiet and rest."

To be able to support each other's authenticity, you need to understand the basis for each other's behavior. You need to understand that your spouse is not directing a particular mood *against* you but expressing it *to* you. Each partner needs to keep the other informed about the reasons for moods and behavior.

3. *Be sensitive to your spouse's needs as well as your own.* Your spouse is not God—he or she can't meet your every need. There are times when you may feel down but your spouse needs you to feel upbeat, when you feel irritable but your spouse needs you to feel good-natured, and so on. At times you may need to suppress your own needs to attend to your spouse's needs.

Suppose that instead of seething in silence, Tricia had said to Hal: "You were lively at the party, but now you seem with-drawn. I had hoped we could make some plans for our trip next weekend. Is anything wrong?" Hal would then have options. He could acknowledge his weariness and suggest that they wait until the next day to talk about their holiday. Or if he sensed that Tricia really needed to talk, he could muster up a little more energy and give her the same genial attention he gave others at the party.

4. *Don't use authenticity to excuse offensive behavior.* Occa-sionally in our work with couples, we hear a spouse justify offensive behavior by saying something like this: "That's just the way I am. She knew this when she married me." But the authenticity does not mean obnoxious behavior is acceptable. Authenticity calls you to know and be what you are so that you

can become the person you are meant to be. It summons you to discern between patterns of behavior that you need to nurture and patterns from which you need to disentangle yourself.

Toppling the Barriers to Authenticity

It's not easy to know yourself or to be yourself. Imagine the disciples' frustration and anger when Thomas refused to believe that Jesus had appeared to them. Imagine the pressure Thomas must have felt to squash his doubts and to agree with them, at least verbally. Picture yourself in a similar situation. You are part of a group that has witnessed a miracle. Another member, who was absent at the time of the miracle, scoffs at the rest of you. You have no reason to lie about the miracle, yet he refuses to accept the truth. Undoubtedly, his refusal would test your patience and capacity for being charitable. What do you think would be the chances that you would applaud his authenticity?

Strong barriers—internal and external—block the road to authenticity. Let's look at a few of them.

The Inward Barriers: Defense Mechanisms

Defense mechanisms are techniques people use to protect their sense of self-worth.[3] Defense mechanisms blind people to facets of themselves that they do not want to or cannot acknowledge. As such, the mechanisms act as a barrier to authenticity.

Some common defense mechanisms are denial, projection, reaction formation, and rationalization. *Denial* means refusing to admit to some feeling or motive. If Hal had told Tricia: "I'm not tired in the least. I'm feeling great!" he would be practicing denial. *Projection* means to see a deficiency in others rather than in yourself. Imagine Hal's saying to Tricia: "Why do you keep insisting that I'm tired? You're the one who must be worn out tonight. Otherwise you wouldn't be such an annoying nag."

Reaction formation is acting in a way that is the opposite of how you really feel. Recall the story of Bill and Jan. Bill frequently used humor to disguise his fear and anxiety when faced with new responsibilities. *Rationalization* is giving reasons for behavior that ignore important factors in a full explanation. For example, Bill might say: "I made fun of Jan's being pregnant because I thought she'd be so cute as a mother-to-be." He really should have said, "I made fun of Jan's being pregnant because I was afraid I wasn't ready to be a father."

Often people are unaware they use defense mechanisms. The mechanisms come to light only when someone else helps uncover them. This someone else can be a therapist, a close friend, or a spouse.

Tim, whom we discussed earlier, illustrates both denial (his unwillingness to admit his mistakes) and rationalization (his justifications for his mistakes). His wife, Marcy, illustrates how a spouse can gently point out defense mechanisms so that they can be overcome. Again we wish to stress "gently." You are not a therapist, nor are you God. You can only suggest that your spouse has resorted to a defense mechanism. Ultimately, only he or she can decide whether this is true.

Here is an example of gentle suggestion. A woman who is an active member of her church's Christian education committee projects her feelings onto the new director of the program. Notice the gentle way her husband deals with the matter:

SHE: Elizabeth doesn't like me. I think it started when I opposed some of the changes she wanted.

HE: I've never gotten the impression that she doesn't like you. I don't think Elizabeth expects people to agree with everything she proposes.

SHE: Maybe not. But she doesn't like me. I can tell by the way she looks at me and talks to me.

HE: Maybe she's picking up on the fact that you don't like her and is reacting to it.

SHE: What do you mean? I don't dislike her!

HE: I just noticed that you look more serious and uptight when you talk with her.

SHE: Well, I guess she does tend to turn me off. I'm not comfortable talking with her.

Additional conversation may be needed before the woman finally acknowledges that she is projecting her dislike on the new director. But her husband responds in a helpful way. He does not insist that she admit to her dislike. He simply points out what he has observed and continues the discussion until she draws her own conclusion about her feelings. Once she does, she is prepared to deal with them and change the nature of her relationship with the new director.

Social Barriers: Pressure from Groups

Barnabas is one of our biblical heroes. Every mention of him in the New Testament shows him to be an exemplary Christian—except one. In his letter to the Galatians, Paul told how Peter ate with Gentile converts until certain Jewish Christians pressured him to separate himself from the uncircumcised: "The other Jews joined him in this hypocrisy, so that even Barnabas was led astray by their hypocrisy" (Gal. 2:13).

"Even Barnabas." Group pressure can create a barrier to authenticity that is agonizing to surmount. After all, who wants to be the lone dissenter? Who wants to suffer the anger or contempt of a unified group?

Group pressure has an Achilles' heel, however. If just one other person in the group joins you in dissent, the pressure lessens dramatically. It is still there, but its power is much more bearable. That one other person can be your spouse.

Paula and her husband, Martin, attended a party at the home of one of Martin's colleagues. Paula and Martin were talking with a group of the guests when one of them related a distasteful argument he had about business ethics with a "narrow-minded Christian." Several people joined in with snide remarks about Christians and their bigotry. Everyone in the group seemed to agree with the assessment. In such a situation a dissenter would feel pressured to say nothing, to be inauthentic for the moment.

"Wait a minute," Paula blurted out. "I'm a Christian. I don't think I'm narrow-minded or bigoted. And most of the Christians I know aren't either."

Paula was practicing authenticity. She was also creating possible discomfort for Martin—these were, after all, his coworkers. She looked at Martin as she spoke. She knew he shared her beliefs. Yet she wasn't sure how he would feel about her speaking out. She saw him smile and nod his head approvingly. After some spirited discussion, the group agreed that it was wrong to label all Christians as narrow-minded.

Institutions as well as individuals can erect barriers to authenticity. In some families, for instance, expressing anger, affection, or any other genuine emotion is off-limits. Some schools measure their success by the degree of conformity rather than personal creativity of their students. And, unfortunately, in many churches people hide their true identities and feelings. God calls us to authenticity—to be who we are and to become what God has called us to be. And if God invites us to be authentic, the church of Christ should be a place where authenticity is widely practiced. But it doesn't always happen.

Many church members fear talking about troubled relationships, admitting anxieties, articulating doubts, and sharing spiritual struggles. Instead, they fall into a pattern of pious inauthenticity, conforming to what they perceive are the church's expectations for its members.

Some persons survive such inauthenticity, while others do not. Philip Yancey, who has had a lifelong struggle with uncertainties, survived growing up in a church that "had no room for doubt."[4] Today, his writings inspire and encourage millions. However, Yancey says his brother's faith did not survive a similar pressure to be inauthentic. He left the church, condemned by a teacher at a Bible college in the 1960s who gave him a failing grade on a speech in which he had argued that rock music is not inherently immoral.

Churches vary in the extent to which members feel free to be authentic. Our point here is not to condemn or to call you to an in-your-face crusade against an offending church. Rather, we want to remind you of an option—authenticity with your spouse. If you cannot discuss your doubts, anxieties, and fears at church, talk about them with your spouse. If you feel less Christian by bringing up such matters at church, we hope you will feel more Christian by being honest about them with your spouse.

Value your church for the nurture you receive there. Turn to your spouse for help with constraints you feel the church imposes on your authenticity. An active church member told us:

> I love my church. I feel God's presence there more than anywhere else. But I don't feel free to talk about some of my own spiritual struggles. I can do that with God. And I can do it, thank God, with my wife.

FACE-TO-FACE

Separately, each of you complete the following two statements in your couple's journal:

1. *I appreciate and value these things about you . . .* Before completing this affirmation of your spouse, read Romans 12 and Ephesians 4:25-32. Include as many of the qualities listed in these passages as you can in your affirmation.

2. *It is most difficult for me to be myself when . . .* Complete this statement by listing as many situations, circumstances, or places you can think of.

When you have finished, talk about your responses. How do your spouse's affirmations make you feel? Do you think of yourself in such positive terms? If not, we encourage you to accept your partner's affirmations and live them out. Perhaps in doing so, you will see in yourself the same qualities that your spouse already sees.

Then discuss the second statement. Why is it difficult for you to be yourself in the situations, circumstances, or places you identified? How can your spouse help?

In your closing prayer time, give God thanks for calling you to be authentic. Ask God to help you support each other in your ongoing quest to be authentic Christians.

PRAY TOGETHER

Help us to be ever more like you, Jesus, our example. Just as you lived an authentic life, enable us by your grace to do the same. Teach us to know ourselves. Empower us to be ourselves. And abide with us as we strive for the courage we need to be your authentic disciples and each other's authentic mate. Amen.

4

A Supportive Haven for Becoming

Grow in the grace and knowledge of our Lord and Savior Jesus Christ. To him be the glory both now and to the day of eternity. Amen.

—2 Peter 3:18

We once read about a lonely grave high up on a mountain in Europe. The tombstone had a simple inscription: "He died climbing." For us, this inscription provides a metaphor for the Christian life—a life of continuous growth and incessant becoming. God calls you to be authentic, to know and be yourself. However, knowing yourself and being yourself are not the goals of your spiritual quest. Rather, authenticity is the foundation for becoming, for growing into what you are not yet in order to become what God has called you to become.

CALLED TO BECOME

Imagery of godliness as a life of growth is found throughout the Bible. The godly are like "trees planted by streams of water" (Ps. 1:3). They "flourish like the palm tree, and grow like a cedar in Lebanon" (Ps. 92:12). Isaiah compares Israel to God's vineyard (Isa. 5:7). Jesus calls himself the vine and his disciples the branches (John 15:5). Paul reminds us of our call to "grow up in every way into him who is the head, into Christ" (Eph. 4:15). And Peter exhorts us to "grow in the grace and knowledge of our Lord and Savior Jesus Christ" (2 Pet. 3:18). What does it mean to grow, to be in the process of becoming?

The Meaning of Spiritual Growth

We have known Christians who believed that they were growing spiritually as long as they were learning more about the Bible. But increasing knowledge is only one part of the task of growth. Peter also told us to grow in grace. To us, this means an increased receptivity to God's grace, which leads to an increased sharing of grace with those around us. Christians are called to give grace as well as to receive it. Giving grace demonstrates Christlike behavior toward others. The more

God's grace abounds in our lives, the more we can give grace to those around us.

Spiritual growth involves the whole person. You become increasingly God-shaped in the way you think, make decisions, speak, relate to people, manage your budget, and so on. No facet of your life is outside the realm of God's efforts to bring you ever closer to the goal of maturity in Christ.

Becoming and Your Marriage

"Stay just as you are. I don't want you to ever change." We have often heard individuals, in an attempt to be romantic and affirming, say this to a fiancée or a spouse. Even while recognizing the good intentions of the speaker, we try to point out the unrealistic and the unchristian nature of the statement. It is unrealistic because everyone changes. It is unchristian because of God's call to become. This call involves you and your marriage. The growth of your marital relationship is as essential to your well-being as your personal growth.

In fact, the willingness to grow is crucial to the stability and vitality of your marriage. Consider Leslie and Phil, a couple whose relationship we watched develop for several years. They began to have problems early in their second year of marriage. They had started dating during their junior year of college and had married a month after graduation. Although they had many common interests, their personalities were quite different. Phil was serious, withdrawn, and showed little emotion.

Spending an afternoon alone in the library was his idea of a good time. Leslie, on the other hand, was fun-loving and gregarious, and in the course of a day her emotions varied from A to Z.

By the time Leslie and Phil joined our newlyweds' group, their differences had become nearly intolerable. They argued constantly. Leslie complained that Phil was boring and uncommunicative; Phil was exhausted by Leslie's demands that he talk or that they do something exciting together. Saving their marriage took hours of counseling, the nurture and support of Christian friends, and a great deal of effort on their part. They had to accept their differences and modify their behaviors in order to accommodate each other. They grew in their understanding of each other's needs and in their ability to alter their behaviors to meet those needs. They learned how to relate to each other with more grace and less antagonism. As Leslie summarized it:

> We have learned how to appreciate each other and our marriage as God's calling, how to bend for the sake of the other, and how to use our different styles to make our marriage more interesting rather than more fragile.

Leslie and Phil dramatize the point that marriage and personal spiritual growth nurture each other. "Stay just the way you are" may seem like a loving thing to say, but "Become what God wants you to be" is more realistic, more Christian, and more beneficial.

The Challenge of Becoming

To become what God wants you to be, both as an individual and as a couple, is not an easy calling. As an individual, you are called to become increasingly Christlike. As a couple, you are called to develop the kind of relationship that exists between Christ and the church (we'll discuss what this means later in this chapter). This calling is difficult for a number of reasons.

You Never Finish

The call to become is like the need to do housework—you never really finish. That is why we use the term *becoming*, which suggests that persons are always in process and growth is ongoing. One of the many parables written by priest and writer Edward Hays tells of a group of students who asked their teacher what were the three most encouraging words of Jesus. The teacher quoted Jesus' words on the cross: "It is finished." The puzzled students asked the teacher why those were the most encouraging words. The teacher responded: "Because those words tell you that it takes a lifetime to achieve your spiritual destiny!"[1]

Neither personal nor marital growth is ever completed in this life. We know Christians in their eighties and nineties who continue to attend classes in Bible study and Christian living. Couples who have been married for fifty or more years attend our marriage enrichment groups. Like Paul, they do not consider themselves to have "reached the goal" (Phil. 3:12). Like the mountain climber, they intend to die climbing. They are living illustrations of the fact that growth never ends.

However, they are also living illustrations that this endless task is an adventure rather than a burden. In our experience, the older Christians who continue to study and engage in marriage enrichment bring an aura of enthusiasm to the effort. Their faces and words express excitement rather than weariness. The task becomes difficult only if you think of it as an item on your to-do list. If you view growth as an ongoing adventure with God and your mate, you can take on the challenge with zest.

Some Changes Are Painful

The process of becoming requires change. While we do not subscribe to the notion that everyone resists and finds change difficult, we do recognize that some kinds of change can be painful. "In order to become myself," wrote Thomas Merton, "I must cease to be what I always thought I wanted to be."[2] It can be painful when the demands of growth wrench you away from the direction you thought you wanted to go in your life. Or when demands prod you in a direction you fear or dislike. Or when they require you to let go of some habit or pastime you have enjoyed.

Phil and Leslie experienced the painful nature of change. Both had to modify their behavior in ways contrary to their preferences and habits. Phil learned to break out of his silence and communicate with Leslie. At times he forced himself to talk with her when he would have preferred to say nothing. Eventually he came to realize that he felt better about himself and about his marriage because of his efforts. But this change was not easy for him.

Similarly, Leslie learned to appreciate Phil's need for solitude and to leave him alone sometimes while she engaged in activities on her own. Although she often would have preferred his involvement, she discovered that letting him have some time to himself was the best solution for them. And the benefits were real. A rested Phil was more fun, more communicative, and more willing to participate with her.

Becoming Requires Conscious Effort

When you were a child, you may or may not have thought about growing up. It didn't matter. You grew whether or not you thought about it. There's something appealing about that. As one woman put it, "Isn't anything in life easy? I'm told that I have to work at my marriage. I have to work at being a good Christian. I have to work at my profession. I'd like at least one good thing to just work for me without my having to work for it!"

Her yearning is understandable. We'd love to become more mature Christians simply by virtue of having lived another day. We'd love to have a richer marriage simply by virtue of having stayed together. But we know of no way to achieve anything really worthwhile apart from conscious and sustained effort.

We attended a concert where we were enthralled by the virtuosity of a classical pianist. The man is an acknowledged musical genius. "Wouldn't it be great," we speculated, "to play with such effortlessness?" Intrigued, we inquired into the man's life. And we learned something that surprised us: Even with his astonishing talent, he practices eight hours every day.

If you want a maturing faith and a more godly marriage, you will have to exert conscious effort. Phil and Leslie would not have changed their behavior and saved their marriage without intentional action. Perhaps you do not have a serious problem. Perhaps you have a good marriage, but we have yet to meet a couple with a flawless relationship.

Your calling, remember, is to build a marital relationship similar to the relationship between Christ and the church (Eph. 5:21-33). Let's look at three qualities of this relationship: stability, faithful support, and sacredness.

First, the relationship between Christ and the church is *stable*; it is permanent. Jesus said to his disciples just before he ascended to heaven, "I am with you always, to the end of the age" (Matt. 28:20). The analogy to marriage is clear. You promise your spouse that you will not leave your relationship. You commit to do everything in your power, with God's help, to ensure that your marriage lasts throughout your lives. This commitment involves more than making a verbal promise. It means that you will give your marriage priority over such things as work, hobbies, and friends.

Second, the relationship between Christ and the church is

one of *faithful support*. The church can count on Jesus for support against the destructive forces of evil: "I will build my church, and the gates of Hades will not prevail against it" (Matt. 16:18). Similarly, a Christian marriage is one in which each partner says to the other: "I am committed not merely to staying with you but also to promoting your well-being." Again, keeping this commitment demands more than making a verbal promise. It requires behavior that is loving, supportive, and nurturing.

Third, the relationship between Christ and the church is *sacred*. "Christ loved the church and gave himself up for her, in order to make her holy" (Eph. 5:25-26). Christ works in the church to form it into a God-shaped group of people. Marriage is also a sacred trust, a calling from God to engage in a joint spiritual pilgrimage. The path of this pilgrimage is not always clear, and it's seldom easy. Like two people climbing a mountain by alternately pulling each other up, a husband and a wife can work together to help each other scale spiritual heights.

Becoming Involves Risk

Psychologist Gordon Allport pointed out that it is "only through risk-taking and variation that growth can occur."[3] Risk-taking applies to spiritual growth as well. When you set out to become what God wants you to be, you risk frustration, disappointment, loss, embarrassment, and social stigma.

The following scenarios illustrate the risks:

- You decide to exercise more patience and understanding toward your difficult boss. Your boss doesn't change. All you get is the scorn of your fellow workers for what they see as an effort to ingratiate yourself with the boss.

- You and your spouse decide to pray together daily. You stumble over the words and feel frustrated.

- You commit yourselves to tithe at your church. The church embarks on some programs and expenditures that you find questionable. You think about ways you could have used your money directly to help people in need and wonder whether your giving was in vain.

Such things happen, and outcomes could be very different. The boss might change. You and your spouse might flourish in your prayer life together. You might find that your church's questionable expenditures actually are building effective programs and reaching people in need. The point is, you take risks when you accept God's call to become. And you probably will find that some of your efforts get bogged down. However, other efforts will be more fruitful, lifting you to new levels of spiritual living and your marriage to a new level of richness.

There is also the risk of not making the effort. At best, an opportunity is lost. At worst, the marriage could end. In all likelihood, Phil and Leslie's marriage would have ended if they had remained entrenched in their patterns. Undoubtedly, this is what happens to couples who cite boredom as the main reason for the breakup of their marriage. People become bored with marriage because they stop growing—both as individuals and as a couple. The marriage stagnates as dullness engulfs them, and the partners search elsewhere for a more meaningful relationship. Yet a new relationship will serve them no better if they shy away from the risk of becoming.

The Path to Becoming Is Strewn with Temptation

During the fourth century A.D., a number of Christians lived as monks and hermits in the deserts of the Middle East, seeking spiritual growth in small communities or in solitude. Many stories have been told about their experiences. One involves a man known as John the Dwarf who prayed that all his lusts would be taken away. John told another monk that he had reached the point where he had no temptations and was completely at peace. The monk's response surprised him: "Go and pray to the Lord to command some struggle to be stirred up in you, for the soul is matured only in battles."[4]

Like John the Dwarf, most Christians would probably prefer to avoid temptation altogether. Yet you cannot escape temptation, whether you are alone or part of a community. John the Dwarf's fellow monk made a significant point: You grow not by getting rid of temptation but by facing and resisting it. God helps in the struggle with temptation. God promises to "not let you be tested beyond your strength" but to "provide the way out so that you may be able to endure it" (1 Cor. 10:13). Your spouse can also help you resist temptation.

In fact, your spouse may be the "way out" God provides. Mike and Fran serve as a good example. For as long as he can remember, Mike has had a fierce temper. However, he didn't struggle much with his tendency to fly off the handle until his senior year of college, the year he became a Christian and also married Fran.

Fran told us that Mike had warned her about his hot temper before they married. But she said that she really didn't see it until about a month after the wedding:

> Mike was remodeling the bathroom of our condo and became incensed when he had trouble removing some old tile. He began yelling and pounding on the wall. I'd never heard so many four-letter words in my life. And before his tirade ended, he had put his fist through the wallboard in two different places.

Fran said that Mike's anger didn't last long. He apologized for his outburst and promised it would never happen again. But it did—again and again. "Every time I exploded," Mike said, "I felt that I was sinning against Fran and the Lord." Mike told us that the imminent arrival of their first child made him realize that he had to find ways to control his temper:

> Fran was a godsend. She talked and prayed with me about my problem. She helped me to understand the things that triggered my temper and to develop ways to avoid angry responses. I can't say my temper is gone, but through God's grace and Fran's insight, I now have a handle on it.

A PARTNERED CALLING

Because the calling to become is so challenging, it is a partnered calling. "Work out your own salvation with fear and trembling," wrote Paul. Then, lest anyone should think it was a call to a self-made achievement, he immediately added, "for it is God who is at work in you, enabling you both to will and to work for his good pleasure" (Phil. 2:12-13). We are partners with God in our efforts at becoming.

This partnership also includes people—church members, family, friends, and your spouse. We tend to grow spiritually within intimate relationships, not by going off on lone spiritual quests. Intimate relationships foster spiritual growth in at least two important ways: by intensifying your experience of God and by encouraging you during the dark times of your spiritual life.

Intensifying Your Experience of God

How often do you intensely experience God's presence? The Bible assures you that God is with you at all times, that nothing in all creation can separate you from the love of God, which is in Jesus Christ. But how often are you aware of God's love enfolding you?

A goal of spiritual growth is to increase awareness of God's presence. You can use various spiritual exercises to build this awareness. Distractions abound, however. Demands are insistent; responsibilities are continuous. The world is a noisy place, smothering the voice of God in its cacophony of hectic activity.

Interestingly, an intense experience of God's presence is more likely to occur when you are with other people than when you are alone. Wendy Wright cites results from a survey of lay Christians in which more than 90 percent said that their most powerful experience of God occurred while they were with other people—a spouse or other family member, a friend, a pastor, or a Christian group or gathering.[5] It seems that for most Christians, a partnered effort is more fruitful than a solitary one in gaining intense experiences of God's presence.

Giving Encouragement at Low Points

"Truly, you are a God who hides himself, O God of Israel, the Savior" (Isa. 45:15). We can all identify with Isaiah's statement. At times God appears to be inaccessible or even absent. Prayers seem to dissipate into nothingness without ever reaching the divine ear. Pleas for help seem to be ignored. The thirst for a more intense sense of God's presence goes unquenched.

Discouraging experiences are common, including the experience of going through times when interest in spiritual growth wanes. Thomas à Kempis remarked, "I have never come upon anyone, however religious and devout, who has not sometimes experienced a withdrawal of grace, felt a cooling-off of his [or her] fervour."[6]

At those times of discouragement and waning interest, other Christians can step in to encourage and reinvigorate.

Your spouse may be the one most suited to the task. Vern, a life-long church member, acknowledges that he has gone through a number of dry spells in his spiritual journey. During one of them, his wife acted in a way that brought about a "huge jump in my Christian growth":

> Nothing stimulating was happening to me at church. I attended every Sunday, but I seemed stalled in my faith. Then one day my wife suggested that we get a home Bible study course and work through it together. We've had many lively discussions and a lot of fun working through the course. I think we've both become stronger Christians. And I know it's brought us closer together as a couple.

Support for Becoming

Among the tools available to make your marriage a supportive haven for becoming are patience, encouragement, and celebration. When you use these tools, you say to your spouse: "I applaud your efforts to grow and support you in your efforts."

Patience

Patience is necessary because change is more likely to be a long, jagged process than a quick leap to a new level. If your spouse has practiced a bad habit for years, he or she will probably not shed it in a day or even in a few months. If the change goes against his or her natural tendencies or preferences, you can expect relapses. At one point, Leslie thought that her and Phil's efforts were fruitless:

> We both agreed that each of us would try to be more accommodating. Well, it only took two days for Phil to fall back into his aloof ways. When we got home from work, I asked him how his day had gone, and all he said was "fine" and turned on the TV. What's the point of agreeing to something and then not doing it? I don't think he's ever going to change.

We pointed out two things to Leslie. First, Phil's lapse did not signal that he doesn't want to change—just that change would not be easy. There would be other lapses, we assured her. She would have to be patient with him as he attempted to alter old habits; likewise, he would have to be patient with her as she tried to change her patterns.

Second, we reminded her that everything in marriage is a mutual responsibility. If your spouse agrees to behave in a new way, then falls back into the old pattern, you are responsible for renewing the effort to change. What Phil needed when he disengaged was not Leslie's anger or frustration but a gentle reminder that he was falling short of what he had agreed to do.

Patience, then, has both a passive and an active face. The passive face is accepting the jagged course of change as well as refraining from rebuke as your spouse stumbles, relapses, and falters. The active face is gently reminding your spouse when he or she slips back into an old pattern.

Encouragement

Actually, your spouse needs more than your patience as he or she struggles with becoming. If Leslie was frustrated, Phil was discouraged. When he became aware of his lapses, he wondered whether he could ever change. *Perhaps Leslie is right*, he thought. *Maybe I'll never be any different.* Phil needed encouragement, someone to say to him: "You can do it."

Encouragement is critical because self-confidence is precarious. It might seem that God's call is sufficient grounds for a Christian to respond with confidence. But most of us are like Moses—we doubt our capacity to fulfill the calling. We need a word of encouragement. We need to hear that someone else has confidence in us, even though we lack it.

A woman was asked to direct a research grant in the laboratory where she worked. She recognized that it meant an opportunity to grow professionally and to tackle a project that could eventually benefit society. But she had doubts and needed encouragement from her husband:

> I had two questions. First, is this what God wants me to do? And second, can I do it? My husband helped me to answer yes to both questions by assuring me that I have exactly the qualities needed to be an effective leader and that he would support me if I accepted the task. I could tell he really meant it. His encouragement made the difference.

Celebration

We celebrate the passage of time with birthdays. Why not celebrate the process of becoming? We don't mean a large, formal celebration—although on occasion one would be appropriate. Rather, we mean small expressions of admiration and appreciation for your spouse's progress in becoming. Consider these examples:

- Share a special meal to celebrate your spouse's efforts to practice more patience at work.

- Say how proud you are that your spouse didn't lose his or her temper when offended by an unkind comment at a party.

- Buy a small gift to acknowledge an act of thoughtfulness that reflected a new level of spiritual living.

- Take a weekend trip to celebrate your spouse's first month of sobriety.

- Give an offering to your church or a deserving cause to express thanksgiving for your spouse's act of forgiveness and reconciliation.

When you celebrate, you reward your spouse's efforts and motivate him or her to continue those efforts. Are such rewards necessary? It is true that, at least in the long run, becoming what God wants you to be is its own reward. It is also true that you are much more likely to persevere if your spouse celebrates with you the small triumphs along the way.

Christianity is not a religion for spiritual Lone Rangers. We all need the patience, encouragement, and celebration of others as we strive to grow. We expect this support from the church, and we need it from our spouses.

FACE-TO-FACE

The Holy Spirit always works within God's people to bring about love, joy, peace, patience, kindness, generosity, faithfulness, gentleness, and self-control (Gal. 5:22-23). But such qualities do not develop automatically or without conscious effort. Think about these nine qualities. Each of you select three fruit of the Spirit that you would like to cultivate more fully, and record them in your couple's journal. Discuss what cultivating these qualities involves; then develop a plan for working together to achieve the desired growth. Be specific and include in your plan a date when you will assess your mutual progress.

In your prayer time ask God to help you follow through with your growth plans. Give God thanks for the privilege of being involved in the adventure of becoming.

Pray Together

Our God, you have called us to the adventure of becoming. We are both grateful and apprehensive: grateful for the adventure in spiritual richness but apprehensive because of the risks and the struggles. Remind us day by day that we are partners with you and with each other in this adventure, so that we may not falter as we stride in faith toward the goal of becoming like Jesus Christ our Savior. In his name we pray. Amen.

PART II

PARTNERS IN GROWTH

*My wife, Laura, grew up in a large family
where she learned to think about the needs of others
and care for them. Somehow I missed out on
that important lesson when I was growing up.
But since we married, I think I have learned
to be more thoughtful and more caring.
And Laura's been my teacher.*

—Patrick, a husband of thirteen years

5

Building Intimacy

Set me as a seal upon your heart, as a seal upon your arm;
for love is strong as death, passion fierce as the grave.
Its flashes are flashes of fire, a raging flame.

—Song of Solomon 8:6

Mother Teresa urged the husbands and wives in a group she was addressing to smile at each other and their children. Some participants wondered whether the nun should be giving advice about marriage, and one even asked her if she was married. She replied that yes, she was married to Jesus, and she added: "Sometimes I find it difficult to smile at Jesus because he can be so demanding."[1]

Mother Teresa was right. Strong parallels can be drawn between marital intimacy and intimacy with God. That's why a number of biblical commentators maintain that the Song of Solomon, a collection of poems about love between a man and a woman, is an allegory of God's love for Israel. The Song of Solomon paints a picture of strong love and fierce passion—of an intimacy that is sometimes like rest in green pastures but at other times is like a "raging flame" (Song of Sol. 8:6). Indeed, it depicts the intimacy that many people experience in their relationship with God and with their spouse.

THE EXPERIENCE OF INTIMACY

Think about your relationship with your spouse. How would you respond if someone asked you to describe your experience of intimacy in marriage? Here are a few answers we have received to this question:

"It's having a shared history—unique to us. No one else has had exactly the same experiences. And this binds us together in a special way."

"We're a part of each other. We're so close that it's hard to imagine life without her. It would be like being torn in half."

"It's knowing that I am accepted and loved. I know that I can always depend on him. I had a troubled childhood, but he has helped me become a whole person."

"Just being with my wife makes me feel good. I feel better about myself and better about life because of her. Every day I give thanks that we are together."

Now listen to a few statements people made about their relationship with God:

> You show me the path of life.
> In your presence there is fullness of joy;
> in your right hand are pleasures forevermore.
> (Psalm 16:11)

> My God, my Helper, I will love Thee with all the power Thou hast given me; not worthily, for that can never be, but to the full of my capacity.[2]

> You know, God, that I have never wanted anything but to love You alone. I long for no other glory. Your love . . . is an abyss whose depths I cannot plumb.[3]

> I was driving in my car. And I began to pray—for the first time in years. I began by saying, "Hello, God." Suddenly there was a bright light that seemed to surround and fill the car. I felt God's presence. I felt [God] welcome me home. At that moment, I was filled with the most incredible peace and joy. I knew that I was loved.[4]

Reread the statements people made about marital intimacy. How many of them could apply to a relationship with God? How many of the statements made about intimacy with God could apply to a marital relationship?

Whether you are describing intimacy with God or with your spouse, your experience of intimacy will include many of the same qualities: closeness, joy, fulfillment, and a sense of security. By reflecting on the meaning of intimacy with your spouse or with God, you can learn about the other relationship. The more you learn and put into practice, the richer your life will be because God created you for intimacy.

Your Need for Intimacy

Psychologist Susan Johnson writes that people have an "immutable longing for contact," a fundamental need to be connected with others.[5] Intimacy, in other words, is a basic need, not a mere luxury. A therapist friend put it this way:

> Even when working with a clinical population who by and large have suffered some form of child abuse and who come from divorced homes, I am struck by their tenacity in trying to find or improve interpersonal relationships. The bottom line, in my opinion, is that becoming intimate and committed, although at times frightening, is a part of our humanness.

It's not surprising that disruptions in intimacy are painful. One reason divorce is so traumatic is because it severs a major source of intimacy from the lives of the persons involved. Times of conflict, even in stable marriages, often result in deprivation of intimacy. Remembering a troubled time in his marriage, a husband said,

> For the first time in our marriage, I felt uneasy about going home after work. I didn't want to face another argument or another evening of coldness. I longed to go back to the time when we loved being together, when I felt a sense of peace just having her slip her hand into mine.

Disruption in intimacy with God is also painful. When the psalmist felt distant from God, he cried out in distress:

> O God, you are my God, I seek you,
>   my soul thirsts for you;
> my flesh faints for you,
>   as in a dry and weary land
>   where there is no water.
>   (Psalm 63:1)

The mystics who strive for an intense intimacy talk about the "dark night of the soul," a time in their quest when they can't seem to connect with God. We have counseled with many people caught up in struggle who despairingly talk about God's absence from their lives.

Intimacy lies at the core of what it means to be human. You never outgrow the need for intimacy. Moreover, in our experience, the stronger the bonds of intimacy, the richer your life will be. So how do you increase the intimacy in your life—particularly your intimacy with God and with your spouse? Here are a few suggestions.

INTIMACY THROUGH COMMITMENT

Intimacy begins with commitment and deepens only with a full commitment. When we say this to married couples, some appear puzzled. "We're committed," they respond. "After all, we're married." It's true that when you marry someone, you commit yourself to that person. Yet we have known many married couples who miss out on rich intimacy because their commitment is incomplete.

A full commitment is like the one Michael Downey describes when he writes about commitment to Christ in terms of entrusting rather than feeling an obligation: "Commitment implies joining oneself to, entrusting oneself to, engaging one's whole heart and mind and soul with the person of Jesus in the presence and by the power of the Spirit."[6] We agree. We also believe that entrusting is the soul of your commitment to each other as well as your commitment to God.

Let's examine three dimensions of such a commitment: faithfulness, perseverance, and support.

Faithfulness

Commitment is synonymous with faithfulness. Persons in an intimate relationship rightfully expect each other to be true to the commitment they made. Any breach of faithfulness will erode or even destroy intimacy. Adultery is the ultimate breach in marriage. However, many spouses who have not committed physical adultery are still guilty of a breach of faithfulness. Jesus extended the definition of adultery when he said that lusting after someone other than your spouse means you have already committed adultery in your heart (Matt. 5:28). Lust is a form of emotional adultery. To fantasize about a sexual encounter with someone else dulls the edge of intimacy with your mate. Even if the encounter never goes further than your thoughts, you have for the moment given yourself to someone else.

Another form of emotional adultery is more subtle but equally important: relying on someone other than your spouse as your primary source of emotional support. Consider the man who befriends a woman at work, begins to have lunch with her regularly, talks to her about his dreams and frustrations and concerns, and depends on her for support and guidance. The man is becoming intimate with someone other than his wife. In some cases, the emotional adultery leads to physical adultery. Even if no affair occurs, the man has given a substantial chunk of his life to someone else.

Both physical and emotional adultery diminish intimacy with your spouse. In contrast, the effort to be faithful yields rich intimacy dividends. A husband in a long-term marriage summed it up well: "My wife is just the best friend I have. I would rather spend time with her, talk with her, be with her than anyone else." This intimacy grows out of faithfulness.

You need to exert this same faithfulness in your relationship with God. Interestingly, adultery is a metaphor for a breach of spiritual faithfulness. Numerous biblical writers refer to idolatry as a form of adultery. To be faithful to God is to remain true in the face of claims competing for your allegiance. The importance of faithfulness is underscored by the fact that the first two of the Ten Commandments demand it: "You shall have no other gods before me. You shall not make for yourself an idol. . . . You shall not bow down to them or worship them"

(Exod. 20:3-5). Moses and the prophets warned Israel that God is a jealous God and will accept no rivals.

Jesus extended the idea to include other things as well as other gods: "No one can serve two masters. . . . You cannot serve God and wealth" (Matt. 6:24). You cannot be intimate with God when you focus attention, energy, interest, and loyalty elsewhere. You cannot be a part-time Christian and maintain an intimate connection with God any more than you can be a part-time spouse and maintain intimacy in your marriage.

Perseverance in Every Circumstance

In marriage, commitment means persevering in the face of the inevitable difficulties that occur with every couple—the "for worse" part of the "for better or worse." During those times you are likely to feel deprived of intimacy. This is one reason many people bail out of their marriages or withdraw from their spouses without making a serious effort to deal with the difficulties.

If you maintain your commitment and work through the difficult times, the intimacy in your marriage will deepen. A husband who had been married for nineteen years told us:

> I hate arguments. So does my wife. But we've discovered that when we work as a team to settle our disagreements, we feel really close to each other. Those disagreements force us to come together. We respect each other's opinion, and we make the solution a joint effort. I have to admit that conflict has actually been good for our marriage.

As a couple, you can also help each other respond to challenges of faith and remain true to your Christian commitment. One challenge may be how to explain a world that doesn't always make sense and doesn't always appear just. Why does so much suffering exist? Why do evil people appear to prosper? Why do you have to struggle so much? Such concerns perplex and distress. They can even diminish your sense of intimacy with God for a time.

Work together to deal with faith challenges and to stay strong in your Christian commitment. Remind each other that feeling distant from God is a common experience. Talk about the issues that trouble you and how they might be resolved. Recall how important and meaningful your faith has been to you. Stay persistent in your commitment through the difficulties and doubts. Your faith will grow, and your sense of intimacy will deepen.

Support Your Beloved

The third dimension of commitment is to speak and act in a way that supports your mate's well-being. Commitment says more than, "I will stay with you." It also says, "I will actively strive to protect you, nurture you, and attend to your needs."

When she first asked for our help, Sharon complained that she was starved for affection and attention from her husband, Miguel. When we talked with Miguel, he shrugged and pointed out that she had no reason to complain because he "brought home the bacon" and supplied all her material needs. Miguel was committed to maintaining his marriage. Unfortunately, his commitment did not include attending to Sharon's emotional needs, either verbally or physically. As a result, they had virtually no intimacy in their relationship.

In contrast, Kurt, married thirty-two years, celebrates his wife's commitment to support him:

> She doesn't just compliment me when we're alone. She does it with other people. And she really bristles if she thinks someone is criticizing me unfairly. She'll jump in and defend me with passion. Best of all, I know that whenever I turn to her for help or support, she'll always be there for me.

Just as you evidence your commitment when you support your spouse, you show your commitment to Christ when you speak and act in a way that confers honor upon his name. When the early Christian martyr Polycarp was told to curse Christ or die, he said to the Roman proconsul: "Eighty-six years I have served him, and he never did me any wrong. How can I blaspheme my King who saved me?"[7] Whether in the extreme situation of Polycarp or in the ordinary affairs of daily life, the committed Christian strives to act in a manner that upholds the name of Jesus Christ, which leads to growing intimacy with him.

Intimacy grows out of commitment. But commitment includes faithfulness, perseverance in the midst of difficulties, and a resolve to support the well-being of the one to whom you are committed.

INTIMACY THROUGH COMMUNICATION

What do you need to share as a couple to have a thriving relationship? Any communication results in a certain degree of intimacy. If you're waiting in an airport and talk casually with a stranger near you, you feel a little closer to that person than to the multitude of other strangers around you. But casual conversation creates only a modicum of intimacy. A rich intimacy requires that you share your needs, feelings, concerns, and dreams.

Talk about Your Needs

While the adage "Actions speak louder than words" is true, in matters of faith and marriage, words are as necessary as actions. When you sin and need forgiveness, it isn't enough to say, "God knows that I'm sorry. Why should I have to confess and ask for forgiveness?" Perhaps God does not need to hear our confession as much as we need to say the words. In any case, our spiritual health depends on speaking the words. As 1 John 1:9 says, "If we confess our sins, he who is faithful and just will forgive us our sins and cleanse us from all unrighteousness."

All too frequently, couples struggle in their marriage because one partner expects the other to know his or her needs instinctively and to respond accordingly. This expectation hounded Marjorie and Henry's marriage from its beginning. Marjorie had been a faithful wife to Henry for more than twenty years, but for most of that time she had struggled with a need to feel more important to her husband. Down deep, she believed that his work, his golf score, and even his automobile mattered more to him than she did.

Then Henry had a heart attack at work, and Marjorie rushed to the hospital to be with him. As she sat beside his bed, he reached for her hand and said softly, "I need you." Marjorie, choked by emotion, squeezed his hand in reply. Later, after he had begun to recover, she told him how much his words had meant and asked why he had never before said these words to her. "I'm sorry," Henry replied. "I've always needed you, but I just didn't want you to think that I was a weak man."

Henry's confession renewed their marriage. Although Marjorie relates the story with delight, we can't help reflecting on how many years of shared joy they missed because of their mutual silence. Henry needed her all along but never told her so. Marjorie needed assurance about her importance to him but never raised the issue. When they finally began to talk with each other about their needs, the intimacy deprivation that had troubled their marriage quickly vanished.

Talk about Your Feelings

On any given day, how many different emotions do you experience? Think about yesterday. Did you have a moment of joy? anger? frustration? peace? embarrassment? worry? enthusiasm? guilt? love? How many of these emotional experiences did you share with your spouse? How many did you share with God?

For many of us, feelings are off-limits as a topic of conversation. We comfortably talk about the weather, a favorite TV show, a pleasurable event, or a problem at work. Yet we are uncomfortable talking about how these things make us feel. However, talking about feelings is at the heart of intimacy.

For example, you could confess to God: "Lord, forgive me for shouting at my assistant today." Or you could confess: "Lord, forgive me for shouting at my assistant today. I was really angry and frustrated with her. I even enjoyed blowing my stack and letting her know how I felt at that moment." In either case God promises forgiveness (we hope that you also apologized to your assistant). But in the second case, you open yourself more fully to God by sharing feelings—a necessary ingredient for greater intimacy.

Similarly, you could say to your spouse: "I saw a terrible accident on the way to work today. It caused a traffic jam and made me late." Or you could say: "I saw a terrible accident on the way to work today. I think some people were injured. I was frustrated because I knew I would be late. I also felt anxious when I realized how vulnerable we all are. And I was reminded of how much I love you and how much it would hurt me if you were in an accident like that." In both cases you give your spouse information. However, the second way builds greater intimacy between you.

Tom and Abby operate a collectibles store. They have two young children. Business and parenting consume a good deal of their time, but at least two nights a week they block out some "couple time" for sharing. Abby explains:

> We put the kids to bed. We turn the telephone off. We sit on the couch, and we talk about the last couple of days. We don't have a set agenda. We might talk about how the business is going and about our concerns and hopes for its future. We talk about the kids and about both the joys and the frustrations of raising a family. We talk about our marriage—how we think it is now and where we'd like it to be in ten years. And we always discuss feelings. Like the time that Tom got angry at a customer who accused us in front of other customers of overpricing several items. That night we talked about Tom's feelings and about how to handle anger as Christians.

Talk about Your Concerns

Have you ever taken inventory of how many concerns and worries you have on any given day? What concerns dominated your thinking today? Your performance at work? A problem with a relative? An unexpected bill? A health problem? A friend who's struggling? Crime in your city? Violence in the world?

If you're like us, the situations that concern you probably range from minor annoyances to momentous world events. Yet every concern, great or small, chips away at your energy level and your emotional reserves. And the more you bear those concerns alone, the more depleted you are by the end of the day. This is why scripture tells us to share our concerns with God and with others (1 Pet. 5:7; Gal. 6:2).

As with anything else you share, talking about your concerns builds intimacy. Tom and Abby have not always discussed their worries. In the first years of their marriage, Tom had many concerns swirling around in his mind that he kept locked up within himself. In part, he was acting in accord with his notion of what a man should be—someone who handles his problems rather than inflicts them on anyone else. A combination of encouragement, coaxing, and prodding by Abby gradually broke through his reluctance. As he shared his concerns, he made what was to him a startling discovery: "When I told her something that was bothering me, it didn't just make her feel closer to me. It made me feel closer to her. I didn't feel like less of a man but more of a husband."

Talk about Your Dreams

What are your dreams? What would you like to do? to become? to achieve? Some of your dreams may be within reach; others may be forever beyond your grasp. In either case, share them.

If we could tabulate the contents of every marital conversation, we suspect that sharing dreams would represent a small fraction. That's unfortunate. You need to share your dreams with your spouse. The very fact of sharing, even those that are pure fantasies, helps you to understand each other better and deepens your intimacy. If both of you agree that a dream should be pursued, bring it before God. When you do, you achieve three things. First, you make the dream a shared enterprise and strive to bring it into alignment with God's will. Second, you work as a team to realize the dream and open yourselves to God's power to achieve any dream that agrees with God's will. Third, you live more intimately with each other and with God.

For example, you may be one of the many couples who have fantasized about winning the lottery. You may even be one of those couples who have prayed to win the lottery. Perhaps you have tried to strike a bargain with God, promising to give a substantial part of the winnings to Christian causes.

If winning the lottery is your fantasy, we suggest you lay it before God not in the form of a request or bargain, but in the form of your dream: "Gracious God, we want to win the lottery because we want to . . ." Putting the matter in such terms can help you reconsider whether winning a lottery is God's will for you (keep in mind that most winners are neither happier nor more devout as a result of their new wealth). God may show you how you can achieve some aspects of your dream without winning the lottery. And the whole process will be an intimate encounter with God.

Other dreams may be more realistic and reachable, but they may never happen if we keep them private. A man who had secretly yearned for years to take up woodworking as a hobby finally shared his dream with his wife. He hadn't said anything because he feared she would dismiss it as impractical in light of the numerous other demands on their time and money. But a few months later on his birthday, she happily presented him with a set of woodworking tools, including a lathe. Her gift deepened his appreciation for her and his feelings of oneness with her. All of this wouldn't have happened if he had not shared his dream with her.

INTIMACY THROUGH EXPRESSIONS OF LOVE

Notice that we did not write "intimacy through love," but "intimacy through *expressions* of love." We assume that you love God and your mate. But the degree of intimacy you experience as a result of that love depends on how you express your love.

How do you express love for God? It is one thing to hear the directive to love God with all your heart, soul, mind, and strength. But how exactly do you do this? Jesus said, "If you love me, you will keep my commandments" (John 14:15). To love God is to obey God's commands. To obey those commands is to experience intimacy with God. Here is Brad's testimony:

> For many years, we never tithed. One Sunday as I listened to our minister preach on tithing, it struck me that we were disobeying God by giving so little. Kate and I talked about it on the way home and decided to give tithing a try. We've been tithing now for more than ten years. I've heard a lot of sermons about tithing. I've heard ministers talk about people who began tithing and suddenly their income increased. I think that misses the point. What Kate and I have found is that we feel closer to God. We feel like we're really contributing to the work of God. We didn't get rich moneywise after we started tithing. But we certainly got rich spiritually.

Brad and Kate discussed obedience as a couple. We recommend that, like them, you attend to the commands of God as a couple and seek to follow them. You will increase your intimacy with each other as well as with God as you do.

If obeying God's commands expresses your love for God, how do you express love for your mate? We have worked with hundreds of couples in long-term marriages. A recurring reason they give for a satisfying intimacy is the expression of love through words and acts of affection.

Partners can demonstrate affection toward their mate in many ways:

- Smiling

- Caressing

- Hugging

- Kissing

- Holding hands

- Brushing against each other while walking

- Cuddling

- Saying words of affirmation

If such actions seem minor, keep in mind that even a smile can be meaningful. A husband told us: "Sarah has often said that it really means a lot when I smile at her. At her. Not just when I'm smiling, but when I'm smiling at her. She says that when we are with a group of people and I smile at her, she feels like we are the only ones in the room."

Many items in the list involve touch. An affectionate touch is one of the most important ways to express love. In fact, touch is basic to our emotional well-being from infancy onward. As Dr. Paul Brand and Philip Yancey have written, the way parents hold and touch an infant provides an answer to the crucial questions: "Am I loved and accepted? Is the world secure or hostile?" The authors point out that as we age, "Skin offers us the most natural medium for communicating basic emotions, such as love. It is our chief organ of contact with others. Skin cells offer a direct path into the deep reservoir of emotion we metaphorically call 'the human heart.'"[8]

God made us as creatures who need and are enriched by physical contact with others. Every affectionate touch and affirmation from your spouse communicates love and can help you experience intimacy.

FACE-TO-FACE

Tom and Abby's couple time, which we discussed in this chapter, is an effective intimacy-building practice. We'd like you to begin setting aside ten or fifteen minutes twice a week to reconnect. Minimize the possibility of interruptions. You may or may not be able to structure your couple time as regularly as Tom and Abby, but try! You and your marriage will benefit.

Couple time is ideal for affirming each other and for sharing your needs, feelings, concerns, and dreams. If you or your spouse finds it difficult to talk openly about your feelings, try recapping the day's experiences. Reflect on what you felt at various times, and share those feelings with each other. The more you practice, the easier and more natural it becomes to recognize and talk about your feelings.

In your prayer time, share with God some feelings each of you had during the day. Ask God to help you deal with negative feelings and to enable you increasingly to experience feelings that reflect your faith.

Pray Together

As the deer longs for flowing streams, so our souls long for you, O God. We thirst for you, the living God. Grasp us with your love so that we may grow ever more intimate with you and with each other. Show us how to deepen our intimacy by sharing all the longings of our hearts with you and with each other. We place those longings in your righteous hands that you may cleanse them and sanctify them. Amen.

6

Practicing Christianity at Home

Whoever does not provide for relatives, and especially for family members, has denied the faith and is worse than an unbeliever.

—1 Timothy 5:8

A minister told us how he learned one of the most important lessons of his life. He was in his last year of seminary. In addition to his class work, he had a part-time job and served as the minister of a small rural church on weekends.

I was working on my sermon for the coming Sunday, feeling extremely pressured and harried, when my eighteen-month-old son came up to me and demanded my attention. Irritably I told him to go play with his toys and let me work. Then I turned back to my sermon. I felt a flush of embarrassment and guilt as I looked at it. My topic was patience! *O Lord*, I thought, *how can I urge my people to be patient when I don't even practice patience with my wife and child?*

At that moment the importance of living out his faith at home really hit him. He left his sermon, went to his son, and gave him the attention he needed. "Unless I strive to be a Christian at home," the minister concluded, "of what use am I as a Christian anywhere else?"

THE PRACTICE OF FAITH BEGINS AT HOME

The minister's question echoes in our minds. What use, indeed, are we as Christians if we don't behave like Christians at home?

A *Test of Heresy*

More than one writer has lampooned the individual who rushes about saving the world while neglecting his or her own family. Mrs. Pardiggle, a character in Charles Dickens's novel *Bleak House*, dragged her five reluctant sons with her as she zealously visited homes where she thought people needed moral exhortation. She was oblivious to her sons' hostility, but others could see it plainly. As the novel's heroine put it: "We had never seen such dissatisfied children. It was not merely that they were weazened and shrivelled—though they were certainly that too—but they looked absolutely ferocious with discontent."[1]

What kind of marriage did this woman have? Her only mention of her husband was to note that when family members made their contributions to various causes, "Then Mr. Pardiggle brings up the rear. Mr. Pardiggle is happy to throw in his limited donation, under my direction."[2]

Tragically, Mrs. Pardiggle focused so much on making things right (according to her own notions of what was right) in other families that she completely missed the point of the Christian life. Her actions did not serve God. They did nothing to add a touch of grace to her world, and they thrust her family into misery. People like Mrs. Pardiggle please no one but themselves. And that's an apt definition of sin, not of the Christian life.

What does it profit you to save the world and lose your own family? A seminary professor said it well: "We've had centuries of debate about what constitutes heresy. First Timothy 5:8 provides a test of heresy the debaters have overlooked—whether or not you take adequate care of your family."

Even most nonbelievers take care of their own. Someone who claims to be a Christian and neglects his or her family, therefore, is worse than a nonbeliever. The practice of faith begins at home!

A Reason for Gratitude

The impatient minister we spoke of earlier expressed gratitude for the privilege of being able to practice his faith at home. It isn't everywhere that you can vent your frustration and still be accepted and loved. The minister's home provided him with a place where he could fall short without being rejected, confront his shortcomings without being shamed, and get the help he needed to overcome them. He pointed out:

> I have needed a heavy dose of patience in my ministry. My patience has been tried—sometimes severely—by endless meetings, by demanding parishioners, and by people who don't live up to their responsibilities. I'm so thankful that my family continues to love and support me while I learn to be more patient. Their example hasn't been lost on me. It's made me a kinder and more understanding person both at home and at church.

PRACTICE DOESN'T MAKE PERFECT, BUT . . .

In the world of faith there are no child prodigies, no spiritual Mozarts who, from early in life, flawlessly perform the works of God. Typically, our spiritual journeys consist of persistent small steps rather than giant leaps into ever-higher heavenly realms. Thomas Merton noted, "There is no spiritual life without persistent struggle and interior conflict."[3]

Among other things, "persistent struggle" means to practice relentlessly the essential qualities of Christian behavior such as kindness, patience, and forgiveness. Without a doubt, the Christian life is a struggle. We know of no one for whom such behavior comes easily and naturally. To behave in a

Christlike fashion, even with—or perhaps particularly with—your spouse, requires thought, discipline, and practice.

Do not expect practice to make you flawless. If you struggle with a tendency toward impatience, it's not likely that practice will transform you into the world's foremost paragon of patience. Yet as long as you practice, you continue to grow. In addition, practice yields two other important benefits: It hones your spiritual skills, and it is a way for you to say yes to God and your spouse.

Practice Hones Your Spiritual Skills

The minister who snapped at his toddler has become more patient by making an effort to restrain his irritation in trying circumstances. Sometimes his efforts have failed, as he freely admits, and he has regressed to an impatient outburst. He continues to practice, and his skill grows.

Just how does one practice Christian qualities? If we urged you to practice the piano or your golf swing, you would know what to do. Practicing Christian qualities is similar to practicing a skill in two ways. First, you need a model to imitate. For piano or golf, the model may be a recording, a video, or a teacher. For Christian qualities, the models are Christ and the teachings of scripture.

Second, you need to devote time and attention to the task. Practicing Christian qualities requires vigilance, a mind-set ready to pounce on every situation with the attitude: "I am a

Christian. How do I respond to this as a Christian?" If you ask such questions, God has your attention and can help you respond in a Christian manner. The more you practice Christian qualities, the more they become a part of your instinctive response.

Practice Says Yes to God and Spouse

When you practice Christian qualities, you are saying yes to God. You are saying: "I belong to you. I am trying to obey you. I am striving to be more Christlike." When you practice these qualities at home, you are saying yes to your spouse and family: "I am committed to you. I am trying to care for you. I am striving to be a good spouse and parent."

When you and your spouse say yes to each other, you strengthen your capacity to cope with the challenges and crises of marriage. A woman moved into a new home, met her neighbor, and remarked about the beautiful evergreen tree in the neighbor's front yard. The couple had planted the tree years before serious difficulties threatened their marriage. "My husband planted the young tree," the neighbor said, "and we agreed that if the tree lived, we would stay together. But if it died, we would get a divorce." The neighbor smiled. "We caught each other carrying water to the tree. This made us realize how much we both wanted our marriage to make it." Watering the tree was their way of saying yes to each other, and it enabled their marriage to survive and eventually to thrive.

The willingness to practice and hone your Christian skills is also a way of saying yes, as Ted and Pam illustrate. Ted and Pam's marriage was in trouble because of his sharp tongue. When things were not going well, Ted berated Pam and blamed her for his difficulties. We worked with them to help Ted react differently. He needed to learn how to control his words and to stop making Pam the scapegoat for his problems. At one point, Pam said with a touch of despair: "I don't know if it's going to work. He'll still blame me and put me down."

"Do his put-downs happen as often as they used to?" we asked. She admitted that they did not. "Then he's making progress," we pointed out. "And by trying to act differently, he shows that he really wants this marriage to work." Pam agreed. It took longer than she would have preferred, but knowing how much Ted was trying enabled her to stick with him. Despite some lapses, Ted's efforts said yes to her.

As Ted and Pam discovered, cultivating the qualities of Christlike behavior enriches a marriage. Let's take a closer look at three of these qualities—kindness, having the mind of Christ, and forgiveness.

BE KIND TO ONE ANOTHER

Get rid of such things as bitterness and anger, Paul admonished, "and be kind to one another" (Eph. 4:32). In the New Testament, the Greek word *chrestos* is translated as "good" or "kind." Jesus used this word when he said that God is "kind to the ungrateful and the wicked" (Luke 6:35). The writer of First Peter used this word to describe God when he reminded us that we have "tasted that the Lord is good" (1 Pet. 2:2-3). Other writers also speak of God as kind. To be *chrestos* is to take on one of the qualities of God.

Kindness Is Proactive

What does it mean to be kind? One way to answer this question is to consider what it means to be unkind. People are unkind when they are mean-spirited and act in a way that harms others. Words and behaviors that debase are acts of unkindness; insensitivity and indifference are too. A spouse who acts unconcerned can cause just as much pain as one who is abusive.

To be kind means you must relate to your spouse in the way God relates to humans. When you are kind, you treat your spouse as someone you respect, care about, and want to serve. And like God, you do not wait until you are asked. It was, after all, while we were still enemies that God reconciled us through the death of Christ (Rom. 5:10). God's kindness means that God is proactive. God takes the initiative.

Similarly, your kindness means that you are proactive. You take the initiative in actions that serve your spouse. And you do them in a way that communicates respect and caring.

Kindness Is a Hand, Not a Fist

We like to depict kindness as a hand rather than a fist. The "fist" approach to serving involves coercion or harshness. Before Ted began curbing his caustic tongue, he once lambasted Pam for forgetting to have the carpet cleaned. "Did you also forget," he shouted at her, "that we're having company next weekend? Is this the way you want the rug to look when they come? Don't you have any more pride than that?"

Ted tried to justify his words by saying that they were for Pam's own good. She needed to be more responsible about household matters. "Sometimes you have to scream at Pam to get through to her," he explained. This comment ignored the fact that he usually screamed at her and that he was serving his angry needs rather than her need for support and patience.

The "hand" approach to serving is modeled after God's act of kindness in sending Christ to a world awash with sin and rebellion. Sensitive to people's needs and concerned for their well-being, God took the initiative.

Gretchen used the "hand" approach with her husband, Richard, when he was writing his first novel. Richard aspired to be a novelist but worked a day job while he pursued his craft. He published a few short stories and then began to write a novel. Completing it took him two years. When he finished, he packaged it carefully and sent it to a publisher:

> Then I settled back for the agonizing wait. I was relieved when I didn't get a quick rejection. My hopes rose. I came

home from work one day to an empty house. Gretchen had taken our son to a birthday party. I knew she would be gone for a while. I went into my study and saw a package on my desk. I knew what it was before I even picked it up. My novel had been rejected. I felt a crushing sense of despair. I slumped down in my chair and just stared at the unopened package. Then I saw a note on top. It was from Gretchen. It simply read: "Remember, I love you."

The note softened the sharp edge of Richard's despair. Encouraged by a loving wife and son, he continued his writing efforts and has become a published novelist.

Gretchen could have responded in other ways. She could have waited until she returned home to see if Richard needed any support. But she didn't. She could have attempted to jolt him out of his gloom with sharp words: "Don't get depressed. The world hasn't come to an end. Take it like a man." But she didn't. Instead she was proactive, sensitive to the hopes of her husband and concerned about his feelings. In a simple act of kindness, she let him know that the rejection had not made him one whit smaller in her estimation.

An act of kindness adds a touch of splendor to your spouse's day. A series of similar acts woven into the fabric of your relationship can contribute to a richly textured marriage that lasts a lifetime.

LET THE MIND OF CHRIST BE IN YOU

People often ask, "What can I do to build a happy marriage?" That's a vital question, but we urge you to ask an additional question: What patterns of thinking might improve my marriage? In a quality marriage, the way you think is as important as your actions.

Jesus stressed the importance of thoughts when he said that thinking about committing adultery was as damaging as actually committing adultery. Paul affirmed the importance of what we think when he exhorted us to reflect on things that are true, honorable, just, pure, pleasing, commendable, excellent, and worthy of praise (Phil. 4:8). To have the mind of Christ is to avoid destructive thinking patterns—toxic thinking—and to cultivate healthy patterns that reflect Paul's admonition.

Avoid Toxic Thinking

Many couples forget that thinking is a vital part of practicing Christianity at home, and they slip into unhealthy thought patterns. Consider how toxic thinking affected Rex and Diana. Rex, an accountant, and Diana, a stay-at-home mother, have three young children. Years of unhealthy thinking had squeezed the vitality from their relationship. Listen to a typical conversation between Rex and Diana. Their unspoken thoughts appear in brackets.

REX: "Shall I clean up the dinner dishes?" [*As usual, she's leaving the kitchen in a mess. She has no consideration for the way I like the house to look.*]

DIANA: "I'll take care of them later." [*He's comparing me to his mother again. Of course, her kitchen is always spotless, so I just don't measure up.*]

Rex (irritably): "Wouldn't it be easier if one of us did the dishes now?" [*She wouldn't do them tonight at all if I hadn't said something. My needs don't count.*]

DIANA (sharply): "I said I'll take care of them. You just watch TV or read." [*I wish for once he wouldn't bug me about the way I keep the house. He doesn't understand what it's like to take care of three small kids.*]

In many conversations neither Rex nor Diana openly expressed what he or she really was thinking. Rex thought that Diana was a second-rate housekeeper and insensitive to his desires; Diana thought that Rex was a spoiled perfectionist who expected a superwoman for a wife. These thoughts affected how they talked to and felt about each other. Diana typically interpreted Rex's offers to help as a put-down. At times, however, he just wanted to lighten her workload. If Diana refused his offer, Rex interpreted her refusal as indifference to the house and his feelings. But sometimes she wanted only to show him that she could measure up to his expectations.

Rex and Diana didn't realize that they were not thinking with the mind of Christ, that instead they had fallen into a pattern of toxic thinking. They needed intensive counseling to understand how their destructive way of thinking sabotaged their relationship. As Rex and Diana learned, you can't change or avoid a pattern of thinking if you don't know it exists. Once they understood their underlying thoughts, they began to change their patterns.

We will look at some ways of thinking that reflect the mind of Christ. But before we do, let's examine a few of the common types of toxic thinking that block you from thinking with the mind of Christ.

1. *Blaming.* Amy always blamed her husband, James, when life didn't go as smoothly as she wished. If the children were noisy, if the gas tank in the car wasn't filled, if the checkbook didn't balance, if their sex life didn't meet her expectations, then James was to blame. He either had done something wrong or hadn't done what needed to be done to keep Amy's life functioning perfectly.

Instead of looking for other explanations for her plight of the moment, Amy invariably knew who was at fault—James. It didn't occur to her that she could fill up the car with gas or balance the checkbook. If these things were not done, she assumed James had failed her.

Because of this mind-set, Amy looked for evidence of James's failures and usually managed to come up with a long list of grievances. Clearly, James and Amy's relationship was troubled.

2. *Assuming negative rather than positive outcomes.* The problems in James and Amy's marriage did not result solely from her

habitual way of thinking. James responded to Amy with his own set of toxic thoughts—primarily with the thought: *You'll never stop nagging me.*

Every time Amy complained about something he did or didn't do, James had thoughts like these: *She's a spoiled brat; she thinks only about herself and about how things affect her. Her mother indulged her as a child and made her think that she was the center of the universe. She's hopeless. She'll never be any different.*

The result was that James tuned out most of Amy's complaints and never considered how he contributed to their problems. Most important, he never tried to help Amy see how her negativity was destroying their relationship or to find ways to change her behavior.

As we shall discuss in the next chapter, change is an important ingredient of success in stable, happy marriages. Partners help each other change. This wasn't possible for James because he thought that Amy's behavior was set in concrete. Even if you don't articulate it, your partner will pick up on such an expectation, and it will become a self-fulfilling prophecy.

3. *Imputing negative rather than positive motivations*, such as: "You don't care about my feelings," or "You always criticize/hurt me/put me down." Jackie's marriage suffered from this kind of thinking. Jackie was extremely sensitive to Devon's every comment—even the most benign. One night she remarked about how weary she was, and he told her she should spend fewer hours at the office. Devon thought his words expressed con-

cern, but Jackie heard them differently. She thought that he was criticizing her for spending too little time taking care of the house and doing things for him. She replied hotly that she had no alternative. He responded, "There are always alternatives." "See," she retorted, "you're always criticizing me."

This conversation is fairly typical for Jackie and Devon. She constantly monitors his comments, looking for a hint of criticism or displeasure. Her toxic thinking has become a barrier to intimacy.

4. *Assuming that your mate doesn't understand you.* Jackie is also caught in this toxic trap. In addition to attributing many of Devon's comments to negative motives, she thinks he doesn't understand her. When Jackie accused Devon of criticizing her, Devon angrily replied that she had misinterpreted everything he said and that this proved she was working too much. Instead of pursuing the issue, Jackie lapsed into a hurt silence and, as usual, said to herself: "He just doesn't understand me."

She was not treating Devon fairly. He did understand that Jackie was weary. He understood her frustration with trying to meet the competing demands in her life. However, he didn't agree that his comments were critical or unfeeling or that she had no alternatives. He simply wanted to explore ways to ease the pressure. And this is an important point: Don't assume your mate doesn't understand you simply because he or she doesn't agree with you or doesn't feel the same way you do about a certain issue.

Of course, at times your spouse may not understand you. An easy way to assess this is to ask your spouse to state the matter from your point of view. Don't just assume that you are misunderstood. This results in toxic thinking, not thinking with the mind of Christ, and eventually it will corrode your marriage.

Cultivate the Mind of Christ

As you think with the mind of Christ, you enhance the quality of your marriage. Earlier we told you how Rex and Diana's toxic thinking corroded their marriage. In an effort to break them of this destructive habit, we encouraged them to monitor and alter their thought patterns. With patient effort, they did. Now if Rex offers to help around the house, Diana does not automatically think of it as criticism; instead, she sees it as an expression of love. If negative thoughts persist, she confronts Rex directly: "Are you doing that because you want to help or because you think I'm not doing my job?" Rex, in turn, does not automatically blame every mess around the house on Diana's lack of care. He reminds himself of her busy schedule.

Diana and Rex not only think differently now; they also feel and act differently. Rex makes it a point to tell Diana how much he appreciates her efforts as a homemaker, and she verbalizes her love and concern for him. These verbal expressions help them maintain a healthier, more Christlike way of thinking.

Here are six characteristics of the kind of Christian thinking that builds and maintains a happy marriage:

1. *Assume the best.* Rex and Diana had developed the toxic pattern of assuming the worst, of putting a negative spin on everything. If you and your spouse have fallen into this way of thinking, learn to give each other the benefit of the doubt. For example, view his criticism as an attempt to help rather than a put-down. Decide that her sharp response reflects your wife's transient state of irritability rather than a rejection of you.

2. *Inquire.* Let's be realistic. Sometimes your negative thoughts are correct—your spouse's remark really is a put-down. However, toxic thinkers assume wrongdoing even when it isn't intended. If you have negative thoughts, investigate. Ask yourself why you reacted negatively and what other meanings your spouse's words or actions might have. If you're still troubled, check with your spouse to see if your negative thoughts are accurate. You may find that you are misinterpreting or overreacting.

3. *Expect good outcomes.* For the first few years of their marriage, every time Jane and Ken argued, she had the same toxic thought: *This marriage is doomed. There's no hope for our future together.* Instead of sharing her thoughts with Ken, she tended to withdraw. Eventually Jane recognized that she had a problem with conflict. She hated arguments, thought they were unchristian, and automatically assumed that they indicated a troubled relationship.

Jane learned to think differently. Now when she and Ken argue, she reminds herself that conflict can be good for their marriage and that people who never disagree simply may not care enough about each other to argue.

4. *Focus on your spouse's good qualities.* You're married to a flawed person. So is your spouse. Each can focus on ways in which the other is deficient and falls short of the ideal, a toxic way of thinking. Or you can focus on your spouse's positive qualities. A wife told us that she reminds herself of her mate's good points when they are in the middle of a disagreement: "It really helps to keep the argument from getting out of control."

5. *Define differences as good.* In the play *My Fair Lady*, Henry Higgins sings: "Why can't a woman be more like a man?" Have you ever wondered why your spouse couldn't be more like you? More responsible? More outgoing? More attentive to details? More punctual? Toxic thinkers define such differences in their spouses as serious shortcomings. Healthy Christian thinkers define these differences as potentially good.

We encourage couples to use their differences for their mutual enrichment. If one spouse is a saver and the other a spender, the saver can help the spender learn to be more responsible about money management. The spender, on the other hand, can help the saver learn to loosen up and learn the joy of giving.

6. *Practice the loving presence of your spouse.* Some people rarely think about their spouses when they are apart. Or if they do, they think primarily about their mates' defects and defi-

ciencies. These are toxic patterns. Those who think with the mind of Christ spend time reflecting on qualities of their spouse that they admire, respect, and love.

A young husband told us that he and his wife set a time every day they're apart when each will think about the other: "We know that when 3:15 rolls around this afternoon, I'll be thinking of Barb and she'll be thinking of me. This keeps us connected." We encourage you to do the same. Spend time practicing the loving presence of your spouse and thanking God for bringing you together. This practice can eliminate the toxic and build the healthy Christian thinking needed to make your marriage a joyous adventure of love.

PRACTICE FORGIVENESS RELENTLESSLY

Forgiveness opens the door to intimacy. Through forgiveness we become the children of God and begin our journey toward greater intimacy with God. Through forgiveness we break the barriers to intimacy—the frustration, disappointment, anger, and hurt that continue to arise in marriage and other relationships. Perhaps this is why forgiveness is at the heart of God—why, throughout human history, God has offered forgiveness relentlessly to humankind. And why Jesus tells us that we, too, must be relentless in forgiving one another (Matt. 18:21-22).

In our work with troubled marriages, we have too often encountered one or both partners who stubbornly cling to their hurt, refusing to forgive. We are not suggesting that forgiveness is easy. Yet we who have been forgiven so much should consider it a privilege to forgive the mate whom God has given us. We need to forgive everything from the small hurt (such as the harsh word spoken in anger) to the deeper hurt (such as a long-running battle over the division of labor in the home).

Barriers to Forgiveness

God calls Christians to forgive. And most of us acknowledge that forgiveness is essential to strong, intimate relationships. Why, then, do we find it so difficult?

A number of barriers impede forgiveness in marriage. One common barrier is the desire to punish your spouse. You have been hurt, and you want your spouse to suffer the same hurt. So you hold on to your anger and make him or her pay.

A second barrier is a lack of regret on the part of your spouse. How can you forgive someone who isn't sorry for having wronged you? Actually, as we discuss later in the chapter, you can.

A third barrier is the fear of being hurt again. What if your forgiveness leads to reconciliation and renewed intimacy but doesn't lead to change in the other person? You then make yourself vulnerable again to the same kind of hurt.

A fourth barrier for many people is misconceptions about forgiveness. They think forgiveness means forgetting the hurtful incident. Or that forgiveness excuses or trivializes the hurtful behavior and that it's okay for the behavior to continue. Another misconception is that forgiveness automatically restores the relationship to its previous state. In actuality, forgiveness means none of these things.

Practicing Forgiveness

What, then, is forgiveness? It means letting go of your hurt, forgoing any retaliation, and working with the other person to overcome the hurt and restore the intimacy. It doesn't mean that you erase the hurt from your memory or that you excuse it. Nor does it guarantee the restoration of intimacy. However, it does release you from self-destructive hurt and anger, and it opens the way to reconciliation. Remember, it takes one person to forgive, but it takes two to reconcile.

If you and your spouse find yourselves in a situation where forgiveness and reconciliation seem elusive, we suggest you address four questions:

1. *Have you told your spouse how and how much you were hurt?* Although God's Word commands us to forgive freely, God doesn't minimize our hurt. Neither should your spouse. A careless word, an insensitive act, or a gross injustice has caused you pain; your spouse needs to know that you have been hurt. It's difficult to forgive and impossible to reconcile when your spouse is oblivious to the hurt he or she has inflicted on you. Don't suffer in silence. Let your spouse know that you feel wronged and that there is a problem to be addressed.

2. Do you believe your spouse fully understands your hurt? Suppose you suspect that your spouse doesn't understand why or how much you have been hurt. What can you do? We recommend a bit of role playing. Ask your spouse to pretend to be you and tell you about the hurt. If necessary, coach your spouse until you are certain he or she understands how and why you feel the way you do. Be persistent. Bona fide understanding makes it easier to forgive and is necessary for reconciliation.

3. Do you understand how you have contributed to the problem? It's possible that the difficulty is all your spouse's fault, but more than likely each of you has contributed to the situation. Ask your spouse what you did that might have added to the problem or what you could have done to avoid it. Forgiving is harder if you believe you are totally innocent—a victim—than if you acknowledge you played a part in the difficulty.

4. What can your spouse do to help? Recall that one of our fundamental principles for effective marriages is that spouses share mutual responsibility for all aspects of the relationship. Thus, when you feel your spouse has wronged you in some way, he or she needs not only to know and understand your feelings but also to help you handle them. You have a responsibility to tell your spouse what he or she can do to help you forgive. What will make you feel better about your mate? What will help repair the damage and restore your intimacy? Even if your spouse bears primary responsibility for the hurt, the responsibility for restoring the relationship belongs to both of you.

We hope that most of the time you and your spouse will find it easy to forgive and you won't even need these four questions. But whether it is easy or difficult, practice forgiveness relentlessly. It's another way to say yes to your spouse as you live out your faith at home.

FACE-TO-FACE

Separately reflect on the following questions:

- Do I nurse hurt and hang on to grudges?

- Is there anyone I haven't forgiven for past hurts? What can I do to move toward reconciliation in this relationship?

- Do I have difficulty telling my spouse when he or she has hurt me? How does this affect our relationship?

Discuss your thoughts on these questions.

Now identify and talk about those areas in your relationship where each finds it especially difficult to forgive. Why are these such problematic areas?

Finally, discuss and list in your journal some concrete ways you can help each other to be more forgiving.

In your prayer time, give thanks for the forgiveness that you have received from God and from each other, and ask God to help you practice forgiveness faithfully in your home.

Pray Together

Almighty God, reign over our lives and dwell within our home. Forgive our failures to live up to our high calling in Christ, and cleanse us from all unrighteousness. As we strive to practice our faith at home, give us the compassion of Christ that we may be kind one to another. Give us the mind of Christ that we may think in godly ways. Give us the mercy of Christ that we may practice forgiveness relentlessly. We ask these things in the name of Christ, who loved us and gave himself for us. Amen.

7

Engaging in
Mutual Instruction

Let the word of Christ dwell in you richly; teach and admonish one another in all wisdom.

—Colossians 3:16

If we asked you to list words that describe the roles your spouse plays in your life, what would you include? *Lover? Friend? Companion? Helpmate? Cheerleader? Playmate? Teacher?* In our experience, people rarely choose the word *teacher* to describe a mate. Whatever else they may think about their spouses, most people don't think of them as their teachers.

Nevertheless, in a strong marriage you are both teacher and student. You teach and learn from each other about how to grow as a spouse and as a Christian. It's a way of bringing Paul's admonition to "teach and admonish one another in all wisdom" into your marriage.

GOD, OUR INSTRUCTOR

We learn through instruction. Contrary to folklore, the best way to teach children to swim is not to throw them into the water to sink or survive on their own. All too often the only result from this kind of forced lesson is a lifelong fear of water. Even if you can learn something independently without someone to guide you, that may not be the most effective way to learn. An engineer told us about his first job after graduation:

> The company has the policy of giving you an assignment, then letting you figure out on your own what to do and how to follow the company's standard practices. There are several books of requirements and guidelines you can consult. But all in all, it's the most inefficient way to learn I've ever encountered. It took me three months to do a job that could have been finished in a week with the proper instruction. During my five years with the firm, I've seen other new employees swamped by similar struggles. So now several of us are pressuring management to change its way of handling new engineers.

The child who doesn't know how to swim and the newly hired engineer who doesn't know the company standards are metaphors for growing Christians and our need for instruction.

Without instruction, God's call to walk in the paths of right-eousness ranges from difficult to impossible. We are like the disciples who asked Jesus to teach them how to pray (Luke 11:1) and the Ethiopian eunuch who told Philip that he could not understand the prophecies of Isaiah "unless someone guides me" (Acts 8:31).

It is little wonder that teaching was a significant part of Jesus' ministry when he lived on this earth. Or that after the Resurrection, Jesus sent the Holy Spirit to teach the disciples and to remind them of what he taught while he lived among them (John 14:26). Or that an important task of the church is to teach and admonish one another.

In various ways, God is your instructor, teaching you how to become a more mature disciple. God instructs you by influencing your thinking and feelings, by speaking to you through the Bible, and by using other people to teach you. And in marriage, God has given you a spouse with whom you can engage in mutual instruction.

THE RULES OF MUTUAL INSTRUCTION

We see mutual instruction as a process in which each partner teaches and helps the other one grow into the person God wants him or her to become. Marriage partners need to engage in mutual instruction because most people do not initiate their own growth. Frequently we need someone else to alert us to opportunities, to identify our deficiencies, and to suggest new responses. As a husband said, "I didn't even realize I was often gruff with people until my wife pointed this out to me."

For mutual instruction to be effective, you need to follow two rules. First, keep it consistently positive. Second, be realistic about what you can and can't achieve.

Mutual Instruction Is Positive

Mutual instruction is positive in objectives and manner. Rather than eliminate a particular behavior, mutual instruction seeks to replace the offending behavior with a preferred one. It aims to contribute to the growth of each spouse and to the well-being of the relationship. The principle of gentle persuasion Paul laid out in Galatians 6:1 lies at the heart of mutual instruction. Every effort to help your spouse should send the message: "I love you. I believe that what I am suggesting will benefit you and will mean a great deal to me. Would you be willing to try?"

Positive instruction is enormously important, for there are inappropriate and even damaging ways to try to bring about change. Consider each of these statements:

1. "You always blame me when something goes wrong."

2. "Stop being so insensitive."

3. "You ought to be nicer to my mother."

4. "You're so dense when it comes to balancing the checkbook."

5. "You shouldn't feel that way."

Unless you're unusual, you have probably made similar statements to your spouse. You've also probably heard your spouse make comments like these. We hope that you've noted the ineffectiveness of such statements in promoting growth.

The first statement overgeneralizes. Words like *always* and *never* are rarely accurate and tend to cause resentment. The likely result will be an argument over the truth of the statement containing *always* or *never*.

The second statement is a command. You cannot force your spouse to change. Becoming more sensitive is not a matter of flicking a switch but of learning new patterns of behavior. Your spouse needs encouragement and guidance instead of an order.

The third statement moralizes. We all tend to get defensive when someone tells us we "ought" to do something. A spouse will likely respond to this statement with a list of reasons why your mother is unlovable rather than try to become more loving.

The fourth statement ridicules. A spouse will probably not respond: "Gee, you're right. I'd better sharpen my accounting skills." Instead, the likely response will be, "Why are you putting me down?"

And the fifth statement tends to create feelings of guilt or inadequacy about the emotions your spouse is experiencing. Even if anger or frustration is not the most appropriate reaction to a situation, a person can't stop feeling that way simply because someone says it's wrong.

Although badly worded, each of the five previous statements may reflect a situation in which growth is needed. How would you rephrase each statement using the techniques of mutual instruction? Here are our suggestions:

1. "Sometimes when we argue I get the feeling that you think that it's all my fault. I'm sure I'm misreading you, but I need to know if this is how you feel."

2. "I know you don't mean to be insensitive, but sometimes you come across that way. Could I make a few suggestions?"

3. "I know my mom can be difficult, but I have learned to accept her for who she is and to be grateful for all she has done for me. I'll try to help you see her good points, and perhaps you can come to appreciate her too."

4. "I'd like for both of us to get a better handle on the way we handle our family accounts. Let's explore some ways we can do this."

5. "Why do you think you feel that way? What can I do to help?"

These statements lay the basis for growth. They neither accuse nor threaten. Instead they express concern, sensitivity, and a willingness to help.

Keeping Mutual Instruction Realistic

Mutual instruction, then, is a prime tool for growth in marriage. Your efforts at instruction need to be realistic, however. There are limits to what you can accomplish. To keep mutual instruction realistic, ask four questions about any particular growth effort. First, is this an effort to change something that is beyond my spouse's capacity? Second, will this effort draw us closer together? Third, is this effort important to my spouse's becoming, or is it more for my convenience or preference? Fourth, what can I do if my spouse doesn't respond to my attempts to help? Let's consider each question.

1. *Is this an effort to change a behavior or habit that is beyond my spouse's capacity to alter?* Basic personality traits top this category. For instance, you can't turn an introverted spouse into an extrovert or vice versa. Yet keep in mind that while an individual's basic personality can't be altered, he or she can modify some aspects. An introvert can learn to become more outgoing, and the extrovert can learn to be more accommodating to the introvert (recall the story of Leslie and Phil in chapter 4). You can also guide some personality qualities in different directions. The apostle Paul was an obsessive personality. After his conversion, he changed from obsessively hounding Christians to obsessively proclaiming the gospel. His personality didn't change, but he changed radically the way he expressed his personality. What you can't eliminate, you may be able to modify or express in more constructive ways.

2. Will the effort bring us closer together? Dan and Carolyn had been married only a short time when he suggested that they join a weekly couples Bible study group at their church. Dan felt that participating in a Bible study would aid their spiritual growth, but Carolyn was not enthusiastic. By evening, she was exhausted by the demands of her budding pediatrics practice and resisted the idea of another night out. Yet Dan persisted, and eventually, Carolyn gave in and went with him. She participated reluctantly. Rather than enjoying and profiting from the study, she resented the time they spent there. Rather than fostering spiritual growth, attending the Bible study adversely affected their marital bond. In theory, the couples Bible study was a good idea; in practice, it strained their marriage.

3. Is this effort important to my spouse's becoming, or is it more for my convenience or preference? This is a tricky question to answer honestly. It may require discussion with your spouse. For example, Al and Emma struggled for years over Al's serious approach to life. Emma, who has a bubbly personality, believed that Christians should exude joy. She said during a couples discussion group:

> Doesn't the Bible say that joy is one of the fruits of the Spirit? Al looks solemn so much of the time that people probably think we're having problems in our marriage. I know he feels as good as I do about his faith, but he just doesn't show it. I think he'd really benefit spiritually if he would just open up more.

Al agreed that he felt good about his faith, but he expressed his faith differently from the way Emma did. It just wasn't his style to be as outwardly expressive as she was.

One of the women in the group suggested that perhaps Emma was spending too much time and energy worrying about how others viewed her marriage. Emma bristled at the suggestion, but after some discussion, she acknowledged that the observation was true. She was more concerned about public appearance than about Al's spiritual growth. Understanding this, she could accept the fact that Al expressed his faith differently from the way she did.

4. *What can I do if my spouse doesn't respond to the "gentle persuasion" of mutual instruction?* Evaluate your efforts as honestly as you can. Have you fallen into coercive or inappropriate ways of trying to bring about change? Have you made the mistake of overgeneralizing, moralizing, ridiculing, or being insensitive in your efforts to effect change? Using "gentle persuasion" can help if you keep the proper image in mind. Don't think of you and your spouse as potters molding clay. The potter is an image of God. Instead think of yourselves as a pair of mountain climbers, each lending a hand to the other, each making suggestions and encouraging the other as you strive for the goal.

Then exercise patience—pray for the "mellowing effect" of time. Continue to let your spouse know what your hopes are in a gentle way that says, "It would mean a lot to me if you would try to change that behavior." Maybe gentle persistence will pay off. Or maybe your perspective will eventually change. Perhaps you'll be like the wife who told us: "Ben's warts are less important to me now than they were ten years ago. I guess I'm more tolerant. After all, we all have our quirks and faults."

The Methods of Mutual Instruction

Think about the varied ways the disciples learned from Jesus. They saw his example. They listened to his words. They were challenged by his expectations that they would carry on effectively after he was gone. We advocate the same methods Jesus used to teach his disciples as appropriate for the practice of good mutual instruction in marriage.

Expect Growth

Don't underestimate the power of expectations in influencing your spouse and your marriage. We recently became frustrated trying to help a couple in a troubled marriage because of the wife's negative expectations. After discussing an issue at length, the husband agreed that he had been remiss and indicated how he would change. With a shrug, his wife dismissed what he said as worthless. "He won't do it," she countered. "He says he will. But I know him. He won't do it."

The wife had reasons for skepticism. Her husband had disappointed her numerous times in the past. Nevertheless, her expectation that he would continue to disappoint her virtually guaranteed that his efforts to change would fail. She had ignored a fundamental principle of human behavior: We tend to act the way others expect us to act.

In fact, we even act in accord with unspoken expectations. A classic experiment by two researchers showed that teachers' unspoken expectations affected children's IQ scores and performance in class.[1] The children whom teachers expected to do poorly tended to get lower scores, while the ones whom teachers expected to do well tended to get higher scores.

Expectations also affect outcomes in marriage. The most important message in noted marriage and family therapist Virginia Satir's book *Peoplemaking* is this: "There is always hope that your life can change because you can always learn new things."[2] Psychiatrist Aaron Beck says that one of the biggest barriers to making needed changes in a marital relationship is the belief by one or both of the spouses that "my partner is incapable of change."[3]

The effectiveness of mutual instruction depends upon each spouse's belief in the other's capacity for growth. Keep your expectations realistic. Do not expect your spouse to grow without help. Do not expect your spouse to improve daily without setbacks or downturns. But do expect your spouse to become a better partner and a more mature Christian over the course of your life together.

Why do your expectations affect your spouse? We believe that in an intimate relationship where the bond is very strong, you sense each other's attitudes. You communicate your expectations by the tone of your voice, your facial expressions, and your responses. Frequently you even know what your spouse is thinking or going to say.

For example, when Cary was asked to teach a Bible class at his church, he initially responded with surprise (that he had been asked) and doubt (that he could do it). His thoughts about teaching the class changed after discussing the request with his wife, Linda:

> When I told her I had been asked, a broad smile came over her face, and her eyes seemed to glow a bit. I knew immediately that she believed I could do it. And that she wanted me to do it. When I told her how surprised I was that they'd asked me, she said that she wasn't surprised at all! Her faith in me led me to agree to do something that has turned out to be a great spiritual experience for both of us.

Set an Example

We were watching our six-year-old grandson's soccer practice. The coach explained to the boys how to take the ball down the field. The boys tried in their fumbling way to follow his directions. The coach stopped them, took the ball, and told them to watch him carefully as he guided the ball with his feet. On their next effort the boys improved considerably.

As is the case with manipulating a soccer ball effectively, many skills are far easier to learn if we see someone else demonstrate them. This idea is the thrust of Thomas à Kempis's classic work on becoming a mature Christian by imitating Christ. We must focus our thinking on Christ, wrote Saint Thomas, for it is "his life, his character, we must take for our model. . . . If a man wants to understand Christ's words fully, and relish the flavour of them, he must be one who is trying to fashion his whole life on Christ's model."[4]

We also learn from the example of other Christians. Each Christian is called to "set the believers an example in speech and conduct, in love, in faith, in purity" (1 Tim. 4:12). By listening to and watching each other, we learn what it means to live as a Christian.

In a Christian marriage each spouse has different gifts and can teach the other by example. Your mate may be better in speaking a word of grace at mealtime. You may be better at responding to the needs of others with generosity. Each of you can learn from the example of the other.

Cary shared a story that shows how a spouse's example can be instructive:

> Linda is an exceptionally generous person. I tend to be more tightfisted—more concerned about our finances and about our financial future. One Sunday our pastor announced a special offering for some families who had lost most of their possessions in a tornado. Linda, of course, wanted to give something. I reminded her that we had recently increased our offerings to the church, and some of this would likely be used to add to the special offering. But she reminded me of a story we had heard a few years ago. It was about a man who

gave one of his overcoats to a homeless person. When asked why he gave away one of his coats, he said he couldn't justify having two coats when the homeless person had none.

Then Linda looked at me with pleading eyes and said: "Cary, we have two coats, and those people have none." So we gave to the special offering. The more I thought about it, the more ashamed I was of my first response. And the more I admired Linda for her generosity. Since that episode, I've been working on being more generous. If God presents us with an opportunity to help someone, I want to respond as generously as my wife.

Use Verbal Instruction

Jesus taught his disciples many truths through words as well as example: how to pray, how to practice forgiveness, how to behave toward someone who mistreats you, how to deal with worry, and so on. Jesus' words offer a prime source of instruction for Christian living.

However, in marriage, teaching with words may be trickier than instructing by expectation and example. Verbal instruction can easily become, or be perceived as, a counterproductive way of trying to help (overgeneralizing, commanding, moralizing, ridiculing, creating feelings of guilt or inadequacy). It should never take the form of a lecture but use the gentler methods of suggestions, questions, observations, and discussions.

Suggestions point your spouse to alternative ways of thinking and behaving. Here are some examples:

"I know my sister grates on your nerves, but when she comes here tomorrow, try to keep in mind that she has really been struggling."

"It seems that we're always late for church. Why don't we try getting up a half hour earlier next Sunday and see if this makes a difference."

"It would really help me more if you would just listen to me rather than give me a solution."

Questions can invite your spouse to think more about how a Christian behaves in various situations. Such questions grow out of a mind-set that relates everything to faith:

"It bothers me that my boss is so unfair and bad tempered. How should I respond to him as a Christian?"

"The minister said we are all called to serve. What does it mean for us to 'serve'? How can we serve God more?"

"I was as angry as you were when your cousin didn't pay back the money he borrowed. Where do you think forgiveness fits into this?"

Observations are comments about behaviors that either fall short of or exemplify your Christian ideals. They note ways to grow or barriers to growth and often invite discussion.

"Monica called today to invite us to that meeting at church. I wish she wouldn't always sound so pious. I feel inferior every time I talk to her."

"Mark is an unusually sensitive person. I really admire that in a man."

"I was thinking the other day about the large gift the Wilsons gave to the homeless mission. They are really committed to that work."

Discussions are a give-and-take between spouses about a particular topic. They are a way to benefit from each other's insights. Here are some topics you may wish to discuss:

- The meaning and application to your lives of a selected passage of scripture

- Appropriate Christian conduct during a marital disagreement (to be discussed when you *aren't* having a disagreement)

- How to incorporate more grace into your conversations with people

In summary, these four forms of verbal instruction—suggestions, questions, observations, and discussions—foster mutual growth because they enable you to take the gentle road in teaching and learning from each other.

THE IMPACT OF MUTUAL INSTRUCTION

Those who heed God's instruction grow in grace and knowledge. Couples who engage in mutual instruction strengthen their bond of intimacy and also become more Christlike in their thoughts and actions.

Gary and Denise, married more than twenty years, wed after knowing each other for only a short time—not long enough for Denise to realize that Gary was, as he himself now puts it, a "chauvinist." At first, Denise accepted Gary's role as "king of the castle." Reared in an extremely conservative Christian home , she thought she should submit to her husband in all matters. She set aside her professional aspirations in public relations to support Gary's military career.

A few years after they married, Gary was assigned to a tour of duty in Hawaii and took Denise along. It was then that he began to realize how miserable she was. While he attended to his job, played golf, sailed, and scuba dived, Denise took care of their first son and gave birth to a second. Her feelings perplexed Gary. He said, "I often wondered why she seemed so unhappy. Didn't she have two beautiful children to take care of and a husband who got one promotion after another?"

The end of Gary's tour of duty in Hawaii set the stage for a revolution in their relationship. He was assigned for a year to an isolated base in Alaska and could not take his family with him. Denise and the boys stayed at their home in New York. Denise described her transformation:

> My initial anxiety about having to make decisions daily was soon overcome by the sense of pride I developed in my newfound abilities. By the time the year was over and we were based in England, I was ready to tackle Gary's chauvinistic

position that "no wife of mine will ever work." I began gradually just by helping out at our landlord's store across the
street. Then we moved to California and I worked part-time
as a Red Cross volunteer. Gary accepted this because his role
as the breadwinner was not threatened since I wasn't earning
any money.

New Mexico was the family's next stop. By that time Gary
had "become dimly aware that Denise was happier" now that
she had an identity outside the home. She took a paid part-
time position at a public relations firm that quickly evolved
into a full-time job. And surprisingly, Gary did not oppose it, as
he would have done previously.

> Denise convinced me that I would be much happier with a
> human being for a mate than a robot. We now communicate
> more openly and negotiate important issues. She has really
> been tactful and diplomatic in helping me overcome my
> remaining vestiges of chauvinism, and I continue to encour-
> age her to further her own professional development.

Notice that Gary and Denise had no intense arguments
about her changed role. She educated him slowly until he realized that his old attitudes harmed her and their relationship.

Both Gary and Denise's thinking and behavior changed.
Neither one considers a woman's role as inferior or subordinate
to that of a man. Both now believe that in Christ "there is no
longer male and female; for all of you are one in Christ Jesus"
(Gal. 3:28). Their behavior has changed accordingly. Denise
continues to grow and to gain confidence in her ability to func-

tion as an individual. Gary continues to work at clearing away any remaining bits of chauvinism and to encourage Denise in her growth. He helps rather than resists her efforts to explore the fullness of her being. As a result, their marriage is stronger than ever. Through mutual instruction, they have embarked on an adventure in personal growth and an ever-deepening marital intimacy.

Face-to-Face

As you learned in this chapter, discussions offer a gentle way to grow from each other's insights. We suggested three possible topics for discussion: (1) what a passage of scripture means to each of you and how it applies to your lives, (2) how to apply your faith during a marital disagreement, and (3) ways to incorporate more grace into your conversations with people. Here are additional topics you may explore:

- How to develop a more meaningful prayer life

- Ways to increase your marital intimacy

- How to cope with annoying people

- Ways to gain a greater sense of God's presence in your everyday life

- What to do about financial worries

- How to get more joy out of life

- God's will for the way you use your abilities, time, and energies

Select a topic (one we have suggested or one of your choice). As you discuss it, keep in mind your fundamental purpose of learning from each other. When the discussion is complete, write your conclusions in your couple's journal, noting what each has learned from the other.

As you pray, give thanks for each other's insights, and ask God to help you follow through on any course of action you decide to undertake.

PRAY TOGETHER

Instruct us, Jesus our Teacher, even as you instructed your disciples when you walked on this earth. And help us to instruct one another. We thank you for the rich opportunity we have to learn from each other. Remind us to hold positive expectations of each other, to be good examples, and to practice the spirit of gentleness. And bless our efforts by molding our marriage and our lives in accord with your holy will. Amen.

Learning to Love

Beloved, let us love one another, because love is from God;
everyone who loves is born of God and knows God.

—1 John 4:7

The bitter cold and the numbing darkness clung to the weary men like shrouds of death as they plodded to the work site under the contemptuous eyes of their guards. Viktor Frankl, who would later found a new branch of psychotherapy called logotherapy, was one of these men. They were all struggling to survive a Nazi concentration camp during World War II.

As they stumbled along, Frankl's thoughts turned to his wife. He could see her in his mind. He saw her smile. He saw her encouraging expression. He wasn't even sure whether she was still alive, but their love for each other was alive. It was real, and it was sustaining him through the torturous days and nights of imprisonment.

At the moment Frankl thought of her, it didn't matter if she still lived: "There was no need for me to know; nothing could touch the strength of my love, my thoughts, and the image of my beloved. . . . 'Set me like a seal upon thy heart, love is as strong as death.' "[1]

On another occasion as the prisoners worked in a trench, Frankl wrestled inwardly to discover some reason for his suffering. He communed silently with his wife about why he was slowly dying in this place. As he hacked away at the icy ground,

> I felt that she was present, that she was with me; I had the feeling that I was able to touch her, able to stretch out my hand and grasp hers. The feeling was very strong: she was there. Then, at that very moment, a bird flew down silently and perched just in front of me, on the heap of soil which I had dug up from the ditch, and looked steadily at me.[2]

Forcibly plunged into a brutish and degrading existence, Frankl managed to survive. The steadfast love that sustained him was more powerful than the relentless hatred that battered him. As the apostle Paul wrote, "Love never ends" (1 Cor. 13:8).

Love Is a Basic Need

We have often asked our students, What are the basic human needs? Among the first responses are food, drink, rest, clothing, and shelter. As they think about it a little longer, our students recognize that even if all these physical needs are met, they aren't enough to make life worth living. Then they begin to name various emotional, social, and spiritual needs.

Eventually love emerges as a basic need. Without love, you may not survive, or at least you won't want to. We read a news account of a twenty-nine-year-old man who committed suicide. He left a note: "You have to have love to live." For him, a life without love had become intolerable.

In the 1990s, the media ran stories about the horrendous plight of Romanian orphans. Infants lay in their beds all day without anyone to care for them, hold them, caress them, and show them through the grace of touch that they were loved. The infants grew into depressed, antisocial children. Even after adoption by caring parents, the children continued to be severely troubled. The absence of love in the first years of their lives so disabled them that many may never know the joy of emotional well-being.

Love is a basic need. Not only do you need to be loved, but also you need to love others. As a psychotherapist pointed out, the failure to "Love thy neighbor as thyself is the basic cause of unhappiness and mental illness."[3] People who cannot or will not love others are, in a biblical sense, not fully alive. As 1 John 4:8 states, "Whoever does not love does not know God, for God is love."

To say that "God is love" implies that God needs to love. This need explains the act of creation; God's need to love led to the creation of humans, who are made in God's image. Thus, humans also need to love and can respond to God's love with their love.

Love is born in the human heart when a person accepts

God's love. The individual seized by divine love becomes a new person, loving God and others (1 John 4:7). Just as God's nature is to love, so the nature of the children of God is to love.

Lest you think that loving comes easily, we call your attention to the title of this chapter—"Learning to Love." Why is love something that must be learned? The answer will emerge as we look at the meaning of love.

LOVE IS A MANY-SPLENDORED THING

In the words of an old song, "love is a many-splendored thing." It is both beautiful and complex. English-speaking people use the word *love* to refer to many different kinds of feelings, ranging from feelings about pizza to feelings about a spouse and God. William Barclay points out that the Greek language, in which the New Testament was written, uses four different words to refer to love: *eros, storge, philia,* and *agape.*[4]

Eros

Eros (sexual love) is the root of the English word *erotic*. Aristotle used *eros* when he said that love "always begins with the pleasure of the eye, that no one falls in love without first being charmed by beauty," and that when you are in love you long for the loved one whenever you're separated. By New Testament times, however, *eros* had come to mean "lust." This may explain why it is not used in the biblical writings.

Although the word *eros* is not used, the Bible recognizes and affirms sexual love in the context of marriage. Paul told the Corinthians that husbands and wives should attend to each other's conjugal rights "except perhaps by agreement for a set time, to devote yourselves to prayer" (1 Cor. 7:5). But come together again, he urged, so that you are not tempted.

Storge

Storge refers to family love, the kind of love experienced between parents and their children and between siblings. *Storge* is not used in the New Testament. But again, the scriptures discuss and affirm the kind of love represented by *storge*. Recall 1 Timothy 5:8, which asserts that those who fail to care for their families are worse than nonbelievers.

Philia

Philia refers to a warm, affectionate feeling for someone—the kind of love that exists between close friends. To the Greeks, *philia* was the highest form of love. But as Aristotle pointed out, *philia* can fade from a relationship as feelings change.

Philia is found in James 4:4 (where it is translated as "friendship"): "Friendship with the world is enmity with God." The verb form appears in Jesus' question to Peter when he asked Peter for the third time, "Do you love me?" (John 21:17). *Philia* can also be used to describe God's love for us (John 16:27).

The kind of love represented by close friendship is a part of your relationship with God. Jesus called his disciples his friends (John 15:15). A friend of God enjoys fellowship with God, appreciates the qualities of God, and desires to please God.

Philia is also part of your relationship with your spouse. In our study of more than three hundred couples with long-term, happy marriages, we found that the most frequently mentioned reason both men and women gave for the success of their relationship was this: "My spouse is my best friend."[5] In other words, those with stable and fulfilling unions liked, trusted, and enjoyed being with the person they had married. The kind of love described by the word *philia* is a central, not a peripheral, part of a healthy union.

Agape

Agape is the most common word for love in the New Testament, and it also describes the love between husband and wife. The Greeks did not commonly use this word, however. Perhaps that was why the early Christians deliberately chose to use it; they wanted to underscore the distinctiveness of Christian love. *Agape* love describes a sense of goodwill toward, and esteem for, someone. To engage in *agape* is to prize another person so that you act in accord with his or her well-being.

Sexual attraction (*eros*) and friendship (*philia*) depend upon the qualities of others. Something about another person elicits sexual desire or the desire to establish a friendship. *Agape*, in contrast, depends on the will of the lover. You act in love not because you find the other person attractive but because you choose to be loving. In short, *agape* means to act on behalf of the well-being of someone independently of that person's merit or even of your feelings of affection.

Thus, *agape* is not a response to your feelings but a response to the needs of others. It is to take the golden rule of Jesus seriously and act toward others as you would have them act toward you. Notice that Jesus calls you not just to *react* but to take the initiative and act—not as others *have* acted but as you *want* them to act. This is not an easy task, which is why we say that love must be learned. You don't naturally or easily act in the best interests of others independently of how you feel about them or how they have acted toward you.

Morton Kelsey, a psychotherapist and Anglican priest, provides a personal illustration of *agape*.[6] On a flight across the country after leading a conference on the spiritual life, he reflected and prayed, asking God if he had been effective. He was answered with deafening silence. Kelsey realized that the plane was flying near the home of his brother, with whom he had never been close. Soon it would fly over the home of his father, from whom he was also alienated.

Then Kelsey contemplated his five-hour layover in Phoenix. He planned to spend some of that time with his daughter who attended college there. He had mixed emotions about their meeting because their relationship also was strained. Kelsey was shocked as he thought about the deficiencies in his love for his family. He realized that nothing would change unless he took the initiative.

He began his new work of love with his daughter. When he got to Phoenix, he focused his attention on her—on doing what she liked and on trying to please her. When she chose some activities that he would not have chosen for them to do, such as shopping, he reminded himself of the reason he was there—to love, not to indulge his desires. While shopping, he noticed that she kept looking at a pair of yellow shoes in one store. He asked if she'd like to try them on. He bought them for her, along with a matching yellow purse. He told her that they were a gift and wouldn't come out of her allowance. As a result,

> Something happened that day between my daughter and me. I realized how much I really cared about her. She realized that I could be interested in her. She could forgive my previous behavior. . . . What mattered was that I tried to love and understand. . . .
>
> I call this the sacrament of the yellow shoes.[7]

That's *agape* love—acting on behalf of another person's well-being regardless of your feelings. Such love is not instinctive, yet you can learn to practice it by remembering Christ's love for you and your call to pass on that love to others.

Expressing Love

What do you mean when you say, "I love God"? You could

mean that you feel affection for God (*philia*). Or that you feel close to God because you are a member of God's family (*storge*). Or that you uphold the honor of God's name by striving to be Christlike in your behavior (*agape*).

Similarly, if you say, "I love you" to your spouse, you could mean various things. You might be indicating sexual desire, affection, a feeling of closeness, the will to act in your spouse's best interests, or all of these things.

Love, whatever the type, expresses itself not only in words but also in your emotions, beliefs, and behavior. Expressing your love in words is important, but words alone do not fulfill the demands of love. Betsy, who was having problems in her marriage, told us her husband, Paul, insisted that he loved her. But everything else about him made his words seem empty:

> I just don't feel the love. I don't see love in his eyes when Paul looks at me. I don't feel love when he touches me. I don't feel needed except for things like cooking meals and cleaning house. If Paul really loves me, why do I feel so lonely, so distant from him?

Paul, a physician, was immersed in his work. His occasional verbal assurances of love were meager fare for his love-starved wife. As important as they are, words alone cannot fully express love. Love is also what you feel, what you believe, and what you do.

LOVE IS WHAT YOU FEEL

Any love relationship involves a wide range of feelings, positive and negative. Every married person experiences episodes of anger, frustration, and disappointment. You will probably experience boredom at some point. At times you will dislike your spouse for something he or she has said or done. You will also share times of closeness, enjoyment, exhilaration, and ecstasy. Such an array of feelings is common for married couples.

You will probably experience the same range of feelings in your love relationship with God. The biblical record is replete with a wide variety of feelings that people experienced in their love relationship with God—fear, betrayal, oppression, anger, perplexity, trust, hope, security, and joy! Few people have been as devoted to Christ as Mother Teresa. However, as we noted in chapter 5, she admitted that sometimes it was hard for her to smile at Jesus because he was so demanding. We know of no one, even the greatest of saints, whose love relationship with God was perpetual bliss, unmarked by any descent into the realm of negative feelings.

Clearly, love is not the source of all the feelings you experience in your relationship with God and with your spouse. The challenge in a love relationship is to cultivate the feelings consistent with love and to minimize feelings that assault your love. Many people find this challenge daunting. Some even define it as a challenge beyond their control, claiming they simply can't alter the way they feel:

"I feel abandoned by God. I've tried to pray. I've asked God to heal me of this affliction, but I still have it. God just doesn't respond. And I can't feel God's presence when my prayers aren't answered."

"I don't have much sexual desire for my wife anymore. She's gotten out of shape since our son was born. The way she looks just doesn't turn me on. I can't help it."

"I'm angry with my husband most of the time. It's gotten to the point where everything he does makes me angry. The way he spends our money. The fact that he never compliments me. The way he gives priority to his work over his family. Even the way he eats. I don't want to feel angry as much as I do. But just when I'm feeling more even-keeled, he'll do something that brings back the anger."

Are these people right? Are you the pawn of your emotions? In one sense, they are right. Feelings such as frustration, anger, and disappointment simply erupt within you. You don't deliberately cultivate them. You may not want to allow them into your life. You may resist admitting that you have them. Yet they always seem to win. Happily, this is not the end of the story.

Controlling Your Feelings

Two important factors moderate the power that your feelings have over you. First, you can deal with your feelings in different ways. Second, you do have some control over the kinds of feelings that you experience.

For instance, how can you respond in love if you are angry about something your spouse has done? You actually have a number of options. You can nurse your anger through resentful silence or sharp-edged words. You can lapse into self-pity, which will also keep the anger alive. Or you can fight the anger by confessing it to your spouse and working with him or her to deal with whatever generated it.

As you learn how to deal constructively with negative emotions toward your spouse, apply the same method in your relationship with God. Say, for instance, you and your spouse have prayed together for something. When prayers don't yield the desired outcome, you find your love for God marred by a feeling of disappointment. You can deal with your disappointment by ceasing to pray, nursing your disappointment and keeping it alive. Or you can deal with the disappointment as you would with each other—by continuing to be faithful, confessing your feelings, and asking God to help you through them. This is a way to battle your disappointment and to restore the joy and peace of your salvation.

You may not be able to insulate yourself from negative feelings, but you are not their helpless pawn. You can decide how you will respond to those feelings, and you can act in ways that either nurture the feelings or bring them to an end.

You also have the ability to control, to some extent, the kinds of feelings you experience. You can't eliminate negative feelings, but you can reduce the number that you experience by attending to your beliefs and the way you act. The more Christlike your beliefs and behavior, the fewer negative emotions you will feel. For example, people who believe that they deserve special consideration from others will regularly experience frustration, anger, and hurt. People who believe that they are called to be like Jesus—"the Son of Man came not to be served but to serve" (Matt. 20:28)—will know more of the joy of serving and less of the frustration of not being served.

Changing Your Feelings

Both factors are rooted in a basic principle: Feelings affect what you believe and how you behave, but beliefs and behavior also affect your feelings. When we were newlyweds, we learned this truth from a godly woman who was dying. She was eager to share with us some of the wisdom she had gained over a long life of serving Christ. One of her insights was this: "Is there anyone you don't like? Do something nice for that person. You can't keep doing nice things for someone and keep disliking that person." She was right. If the way you feel isn't consistent with Christian love, attend to what you believe and how you behave, which will change the way you feel.

A woman attending a single parents group we led told how she had learned this principle. Her husband had divorced her to be with another woman. Like most victims of such betrayal, she struggled with feelings of intense anger toward her ex-husband. Someone told her to pray for her ex every day for two weeks. Praying for someone is a way to love that person. Loving her ex-husband in that way could change her feelings for him.

But her first reaction was, "Yeah, I'll pray for him. I'll pray that someone will run over him with a car." Fortunately, she decided to try it anyway. She prayed daily for her ex-husband's well-being. At the end of two weeks, her anger was gone! And it has not returned. By acting in a way that differed from her feelings, she engaged in an act of love that altered those feelings and became a healing experience for her.

LOVE IS WHAT YOU BELIEVE

God believes in you. God believes you are valuable. God believes so strongly in your worth that Christ died for you. This is the gospel message for you and for every person on this earth. It is a message that flows out of God's love.

To love someone, then, is to believe in that person's worth. As Charles de Foucauld wrote, we must "see the beloved children of God in all people, and not just in the good, not just in the Christians, not just in the saints, but in *all* the people."[8] Believing that all people are God's children leads you to engage in "tenderness in feelings, sweetness in words, and charity in actions" toward them.[9]

When you believe that God is worthy of your devotion, you love God. When you believe that even the persons who make life difficult for you are worthy of Christ's sacrifice, you love those people. When you believe that your spouse is worthy of your wholehearted commitment, you love him or her. And such beliefs, as Foucauld rightly saw, create tender feelings, sweet words, and charitable actions.

Believing in your spouse's worth will save you from the "me-ism" that pervades our culture and afflicts so many marriages. Me-ism is a preoccupation with one's own needs, an obsession with self-knowledge and self-fulfillment. Me-ism goes beyond a healthy concern for yourself; it is more like an addiction. We have seen me-ism in spouses who abandon their family in order "to find" themselves. In our judgment, people usually don't find themselves by severing their intimate relationships.

Me-ism evidences itself in marriages where the spouses focus on the partner's shortcomings and what that person must do to repair the relationship. Frequently in marital counseling we ask each partner at some point: "What do you think you could do to improve this relationship?" Often the response is a surprised stare and a fumbling for words. If we ask, "What could your partner do to improve this relationship?" the answer is quick and lengthy. The individual has thought only about the partner's responsibility for the problems, not about his or her role in creating or alleviating difficulties in the relationship.

If you believe that your mate has worth, you will focus on his or her needs without ignoring or abandoning your own. As a husband in a long-term marriage put it, making a marriage work requires "complete consideration for your partner's happiness and well-being." He asserted that divorce would not occur if both partners believed in and practiced such consideration.

Our research suggests he is right. People in happy, long-term marriages say their partner's well-being is of prime importance to them. As we studied such marriages, we heard again and again: "This is how I am trying to fulfill the needs of my spouse" and "This is what my spouse is doing to fulfill my needs." A husband married for twenty-one years put it this way:

> My marriage endures because my wife has given me a safe haven in which to live, receive care and affection, and grow along with her. I think I provide the same atmosphere for her. You see, each of us has the best interests of the other at heart.

LOVE IS WHAT YOU DO

As we pointed out earlier, love in the sense of *agape* is an act of the will rather than a response to inner feelings. If you exercise *agape* love toward someone, you may or may not like the person. You may or may not even know the person. This is not important. What is important is that you have chosen to believe in the person's worth and to act on behalf of his or her well-being. *Agape* love, then, is primarily what you *do*. What you do can change your feelings, but it is the doing, not the feeling, that has priority in Christian love.

Indeed, whenever the Bible talks about God's love for us, it is in terms of what God has done rather than about how God feels. God's love is expressed in the Creation, the deliverance of the Hebrews from bondage in Egypt, and the giving of Jesus Christ to the world. Because God loves, God acts. Similarly, God's people are called upon to love not just "in word or speech, but in truth and action" (1 John 3:18).

Loving When Life Is Difficult . . . or Not

A lot of things make life difficult. Perhaps a coworker daily causes you stress. Or perhaps you feel alienated from your spouse. Such times call for love. Granted, it may be more enjoyable to think dark thoughts about an odious coworker than to act in his or her best interest. It may seem more gratifying to nurse your resentment when your spouse disappoints you than to do something kind. Yet dark thoughts and nursed resentment are affronts to love. Love isn't always the easy course. It isn't always the instinctive reaction. But it is the godly way. Always.

Helen tells how she tries to practice love even during the difficult times in her marriage:

> The hardest times for us are when we are having an argument. When I'm angry, I can say things that I regret later on. So when Gordon and I argue, I've learned to remind myself of the good life we have together. I think about the fact that he's usually kind and understanding and fun to be with. When I do this, I don't blurt out something really hurtful. And I think Gordon senses that I'm trying to be loving because the more I think about the good things in our marriage, the quicker we seem to be able to resolve the problem.

Gordon has done his share of loving through the difficult times in their marriage. He recalls a period when Helen spent a lot of time taking care of her sick mother:

> She'd come home worn out. We didn't go out like we used to. We didn't have sex very often. I really felt neglected. I found myself getting angry. Why couldn't she just hire someone to take care of her mother? Why should her mother's illness take over our lives? Then I started thinking about Helen and her needs. I knew she felt like her mother really needed her now. And I reminded myself that this was only a relatively short-term situation. Helen needed my support rather than my criticism. I tried to give support to her. Looking back on it, I'd have to say that going through this time together—helping each other instead of battling each other—brought us closer together.

As Gordon and Helen illustrate, love is the godly (and therefore more effective) way to deal with negative feelings and difficult situations. However, they illustrate another truth: Love needs to be a staple of life and not merely on call for difficult times. When acts of love are routine, you add layer upon layer of richness to your marriage. Love becomes the milieu in which you live and move and have your being. Helen sees her marriage in such terms:

> I once heard someone say that love is what you've been through together. I never understood that until now. When I look back on my life with Gordon, I can see how love is the way you deal with each other through all the ups and downs of life. When you've been through so many things together,

you get to a point where you can say, "I know I'm loved. And I know I'll always be loved. No matter what I say or do, I'll still be loved."

Every Act of Love Is Momentous

Every act of Christian love is momentous. We stress *every* because some acts of love are dramatic, while others are quite simple. Jesus stressed the importance of both kinds. He said that something as dramatic as forgiveness should be unlimited and that even a simple deed such as giving someone a cup of cold water in his name would be rewarded.

Acting in love toward your spouse, therefore, includes forgiving your spouse when you feel hurt and supporting your spouse when he or she is struggling. But acts of love also include the undramatic, such as common courtesies that tell your spouse you respect him or her and affirmations that build up your spouse.

Every act of love, whether dramatic or simple, is momentous for four reasons:

1. *It demonstrates your commitment to the Lord* who loves you and has called you to love others.

2. *It makes a difference in you.* Even before the creative word of God went forth and brought all the heavens and the earth into being, in the eternal mind of God existed the plan that humans should become "conformed to the image of his Son" (Rom. 8:29). This conformity increases with every act of love.

3. *It has an impact on the one you love.* In marriage, acts of love build up your mate's emotional capital. They provide the kind of security that Helen knows when she says that no matter what happens, she can count on Gordon's love. Acts of love also stimulate growth. Immersing your spouse in love provides the milieu in which he or she can flourish spiritually.

4. *It adds richness to your relationship.* It adds another strand to the cord that binds you together. It adds another link to the chain of your shared history. And the more frequent and meaningful those links are, the more you understand why "'til death do us part" is an invitation to a sumptuous feast. The chain of your shared history does not limit your freedom, but instead it becomes the garland you wear to a celebration.

A husband who recalled the shared history of his marriage identified an early link as one that impressed him with the richness of his relationship:

> We've had some difficult times. We were even ready to split up once. But when that happened, I realized how desperately I wanted our marriage to work. How I wanted to grow old with her. How I wanted us to be together when our children married, when we had grandchildren, and when we died. And I know I felt that way because of what happened early on. It was the way she loved me when I was struggling with my career. She would hold me in her arms at night. It was her way of telling me that everything was okay. That she was with me and would stand by me. It's funny. I used to think that sex was the most important thing. I can't remember much about the sex when we were first married. But I

remember the way she held me. And I know I want to be with her forever.

FACE-TO-FACE

Discuss the four kinds of love—eros, storge, philia, and agape— as they apply to your marriage. Frame your discussion around the following questions:

1. How would you describe the feelings that accompany this kind of love?

2. When your spouse expresses this kind of love, what feelings does it generate within you?

3. How important do you think this kind of love is compared to the others?

4. What do you believe is the Christian perspective on this kind of love?

5. Through what actions do you express this kind of love?

6. What actions of your spouse convey this kind of love to you?

Next, discuss which of the four kinds of love are appropriate in your relationship with God. What does each say about how God relates to you? How you can express each kind as you relate to God?

In your couple's journal record the answers to these questions. Underline any answer that represents a behavior you would like to work on so you can become more loving. Talk about how you will help each other. Set a time in about six months when you will review the progress you've made and decide on any additional work.

In your prayer time, give God thanks for the gift of love, and ask for the help of the Spirit in fulfilling the two greatest commandments—to love God with all your being and to love your neighbor (including each other) as yourselves.

PRAY TOGETHER

God of love, you have made us as creatures who need both to give and to receive love. Teach us how to love each other and to love other people even as you have loved us. May what we feel, what we think, and what we do be ever more formed by, and ever more reflective of, the love of Jesus Christ, our Savior. In his name we pray. Amen.

PART III

TOGETHER THROUGH HIGHS AND LOWS

*There's an old gospel song my mother used to sing
that said, "Sometimes I'm up and sometimes I'm down,
but I know the Lord laid his hands on me."
That's the way my marriage has been. Up and down.
But through it all, I know God's hand has been
on Rob and me. God brought us together
and God will see us through.*

—Marion, a wife of eighteen years

9

Growing through Crises

I have learned to be content with whatever I have. I know
what it is to have little, and I know what it is to have plenty.
In any and all circumstances I have learned the secret of
being well-fed and of going hungry, of having plenty and of
being in need.

—Philippians 4:11-12

One day shortly after he began kindergarten, our grandson
Jeff came into the house looking weary. "Are you tired
from your day at school?" we asked. He nodded, sighed, and
said, "All living creatures get tired."

He was right. At five years of age, Jeff was already learning
that life can be a struggle. A minister wrote that whenever he
was tempted to become angry or impatient with a child, he
would look at the child's feet and think "of the long, hard,
dusty road" that child would have to travel.

Of course, life is more than struggle. The road is not always hard and dusty. Even the apostle Paul, with all his sufferings for Christ, said that he had times of plenty as well as times of leanness. We'll look at the high points of your journey—the times of exhilaration—in the next chapter. In this one, we'll explore those crisis times in your relationship with God and your spouse when you feel like you are on the long, hard, dusty road.

CRISIS AND INTIMACY

Crises come in all sorts of packages. Some are minor and brief; others are major and long-term. A relatively minor, brief crisis could be a week during which you are so overwhelmed with work problems that God seems remote or when an argument with your spouse turns into a few hours of cold war. A major, long-term crisis could be an extended illness, a family member's addiction problem, or a vexing difference between you and your spouse that seems irreparable.

Crises bring people to the ragged edge of life. In addition to fraying your emotions and wresting vitality from your body, crises may disrupt or threaten to disrupt your intimacy with God or your spouse or both. The disruption both intensifies the crisis and distances you from a crucial resource for dealing with it. As you reflect on the crises of your life, you may find yourself agreeing with a physician's observations about the times that were most difficult:

I've had professional challenges and personal challenges. But as I look back on my life, I think the worst times for me were when I felt distant from God and distant from my husband. As long as I was secure in God's love and my husband's love, I could deal with anything. When I was alienated from them, nothing seemed right with my world.

Unfortunately, disruptions in intimacy with God and your spouse often occur simultaneously, with one disruption tending to trigger the other. Awash in a spiritual crisis, you may become disconnected from your spouse as well as from God. Caught up in a marital dispute, you may feel remote from God. Struggling with a difficult work situation, you may feel alone rather than connected with God and your spouse. Kent, a computer specialist, tells how problems at his workplace led to a loss of intimacy first with his wife, Holly, and then with God:

It began when the company started restructuring. I was demoted. My boss assured me that it wasn't any reflection on my work, only on the realities of the market and our place in it. But it still hurt. I had to take a cut in pay. Holly said we would manage, but I was embarrassed to think that I could no longer provide for my family in the same way.

Then it got worse. The company was going down the tubes. I was laid off. For a long time, I couldn't find another position. Holly offered to get a job, but I thought she needed to stay home for our kids' sake. When things got really tight, she insisted on going to work, and that led to a lot of arguing and bad feelings between us. Then I began to blame God for letting my life go to pieces. So there I was, out of work, fighting with my wife, worrying about our two kids, and having no idea where God was in it all. You can't get much lower than that.

As Kent and Holly discovered, life is a plexus of intimate relationships. Disturb one relationship, and you will likely disturb others as well. Kent and Holly discovered another truth: Disruptions are painful, but they need not be fatal. There are ways of dealing with crises that can turn them into growth experiences. Before discussing these ways, consider some of things that cause crises in people's lives.

THE MANY FACES OF CRISIS

To paraphrase an old adage, one couple's crisis is another couple's opportunity. Only a few situations or experiences, such as the discovery that your spouse has been unfaithful or the death of a child, *always* result in a crisis. Other circumstances—such as the loss of a job; disputes over money, sex, or disciplining the children; responsibility for household chores; interfering in-laws— are *likely* to cause a crisis. We have known couples who had few or even no problems with a period of unemployment, viewing it as a respite or as a time for reflecting on life. They experienced no disruption of intimacy; in some cases they even deepened their intimate relationships.

Some sources of crisis are not quite so obvious and may blindside you. Two of these are especially hazardous to relationships: having unrealistic expectations and taking the relationship for granted.

Having Unrealistic Expectations

Without malicious intent or even noticing what is happening, your preferences for life can become your expectations of others. Thus, "I prefer to be healthy" can become "I expect you, O God, to keep me free of health problems." "I prefer to be happy" can become "I expect you, my spouse, to make me happy." "I prefer peace and harmony" can become "I expect both God and my spouse to keep my life hassle-free."

These expectations may not be verbalized. You may not be aware of them. Yet they surface when they are violated. As psychiatrist Aaron Beck points out, a good deal of the anger that arises between distressed spouses comes from "broken rules rather than from objectively bad actions on the part of one of the mates."[1] All too often, partners base these rules on their expectations of each other rather than on explicitly stated agreements.

Many expectations are realistic and legitimate. You can rightfully expect God to continue to love you and stand by you regardless of your circumstances, for this is one of God's promises. You can rightfully expect your spouse to be faithful, supportive, and caring, for this was the pledge of your marriage vows.

In our experience, however, people also tend to cling to a number of unrealistic expectations in their relationship with God and a spouse. Sooner or later, an unrealistic expectation will be violated, resulting in a crisis, personal trauma, and a disruption in your intimacy with God, your spouse, or both. For example, one unrealistic expectation is this: "I expect you to fulfill all my needs." In a sense, this is a realistic expectation for your relationship with God. The Lord is, after all, your Shepherd; you shall not want. The problem is that none of us can distinguish absolutely between what we prefer and what we really need. Usually the expectation becomes: "I expect you, God, to fulfill all my needs as I understand what those needs are." And disappointment is guaranteed. A more realistic expectation, one that avoids the disruption of intimacy, is this: "I expect you, gracious God, to fulfill all my needs as you understand those needs. I trust you to understand me better than I understand myself."

Expecting your spouse to fulfill all your needs is also unrealistic, although many people bring such an expectation into marriage. It is as if they had taken the vow, "I, John, take thee, Mary, to be my lawfully wedded *everything*." Yet this is a sure formula for disillusionment. As Kierkegaard rightly put it, the marriage ceremony is not a celebration of victory but "a godly challenge, [which] does not greet the lovers as victors, but invites them to a struggle, encloses them in the arena of a state well-pleasing unto God."[2]

Your spouse will meet many of your needs. However, other persons will meet some of your needs and some of your spouse's needs. This fact doesn't pose a threat to your union. On the contrary, it liberates you from an impossible task.

Another common unrealistic expectation is this: "I expect you to make me happy." No one sets a goal of attaining unhappiness in life. Indeed, our culture lauds the virtue of happiness. Advertisers use the lure of greater happiness to sell everything from massages to music lessons. But happiness does not appear to be God's most important goal for people. God calls us to lives of righteousness, to grow into the likeness of Christ. Although walking on the path toward Christlikeness is the happiest and healthiest way to live, this path does not offer bliss at every step. At times, it is a hard and dusty way. If you expect unrelenting happiness, you cannot achieve righteousness. And you will be disappointed with God. But if you strive for righteousness, you will maximize the happy moments of your life, and you will have a more realistic vision of your relationship with God.

In the same way, you make your marriage vulnerable to crisis if you expect your spouse to keep you happy. You are not called to ensure each other's happiness. You do have a mutual responsibility to love your spouse and to work for his or her well-being. This responsibility will sometimes create happiness; sometimes it will produce uneasiness. But your actions of love for each other will give you more happiness than you would have by striving only for happiness itself.

Taking Your Relationship for Granted

Consider the following parable. A couple came upon a lovely old vase in an antique store. They purchased it and took it home. They discussed where to place it but couldn't decide. They tucked it away, intending to find just the right spot for it in their house. However, they got caught up in the whirl of activities that comprised their life. Days, months, and years passed. One day they thought about the lovely vase again. They knew just the spot where it would adorn their home. But they had forgotten where they put it, and they searched for it in vain. The vase was not to be found.

In the same way, if you take for granted the blessings that can adorn your life, you may one day discover that you have lost them. If you don't try to stay close to God every day, you may find it difficult to make contact when you do seek God. If you neglect your spouse because of the demands of work, children, or community service, you may discover that you can no longer connect with each other when you do spend time together. To continue to take another person for granted is to cut, strand by strand, the bond of intimacy. Eventually, the bond will be completely severed.

You can avoid getting mired in the crisis of a taken-for-granted relationship by giving it regular attention. When you pray, you attend to your relationship with God. Many people grow up thinking of prayer as something done at night before going to sleep, but this isn't sufficient for a rich relationship with God. Instead, we need to pray both as individuals and as a couple throughout each day. Begin the day in prayer; then carry on a conversation with God as you go from activity to activity. In other words, include God in everything you do.

With your spouse, you also avoid the crisis of a taken-for-granted relationship by attending to your marriage on a regular basis. This doesn't necessarily mean that you must constantly "work at" your relationship. As one husband told us: "I get so tired of hearing people say that you have to work at marriage. Why doesn't anyone ever encourage you to *play* at your marriage?" Actually, we do. We urge couples to continue the thoughtful and fun activities they did when they were courting each other. We encourage them to find ways to laugh together. To surprise each other with flowers for no other reason than "I love you." To plan an unexpected outing. To write a love letter. To do, in short, the things that say to the spouse, "You are always in my heart and on my mind." If you follow this practice, you won't have a trouble-free marriage, but you'll never face the crisis of being taken for granted.

Reacting to Crises

"Affliction," wrote Helmut Thielicke, "teaches a [person] to pray; but it may also teach him [or her] to curse."[3] In other words, people respond to crises in positive and negative ways. If you do nothing more than curse the darkness that enshrouds you at such a time, you may survive only to find life greatly impoverished. If you pray throughout the crisis, you may not only survive but also find life greatly enriched.

Cursing and praying are not the only ways people respond

to crises. In the next section, we will explore responses that enable you not merely to survive but to grow through a crisis. First, let's look at some counterproductive responses that hinder growth and even diminish the quality of your life.

Three common but ineffective ways that people respond to crises are denial, avoidance, and scapegoating. *Denial*, probably the most common, is refusing to believe problems that others can plainly see. *Avoidance* means that you acknowledge the problem but avoid confronting and dealing with it. In *scapegoating* you also acknowledge the problem but blame it on someone or something else. Only when that someone or something changes will your problem be resolved.

We find that people frequently try to deal with a marital crisis by resorting to denial, avoidance, scapegoating, or some combination of these methods. A woman married to an alcoholic may refuse to admit that he has a drinking problem. She may insist that he stop drinking as soon as the stress at the office eases, or she may believe that his drinking is not much different from that of other men. A man distressed by an interfering in-law may admit to his frustration but insist that he can do nothing to change the situation.

A husband and a wife whose intimacy is strained by disagreement over spending money may blame everything from inadequate salaries to a materialistic culture to overindulgent parents for their problem. Harvey, a clerk in a hardware store, blamed all three:

My wife and I fight way too much about the budget. But it's not our fault. I don't get paid enough for the work I do. Not for the kind of world we live in now. You can't believe how much it costs to raise kids. Last week, they each had a birthday party to go to, and we had to buy presents for them to take. Kids today don't get cheap toys. Even so, I wouldn't spend as much as my wife does. She just doesn't know how to budget. Her parents never taught her the value of money.

Denial, avoidance, and scapegoating have one thing in common: They deflect attention from more helpful ways of coping with the situation. If Harvey poured as much thought and energy into working with his wife to cope with their limited income as he did into blaming others, he could greatly reduce the amount of their conflict. This, in turn, would restore some of the intimacy they have lost.

If you get into the habit of using these methods with each other, you will probably carry them over into your relationship with God. Imagine that you and your spouse feel depressed because of a stressful situation. You pray, but God doesn't deliver you from the situation. The stress continues to pummel you, and with every blow you feel ever more distant from God. You resort to the methods you have used in dealing with your marital crises. You may employ denial, suppressing your feeling that God is becoming ever more remote or shrugging off the stress as one of life's inevitable challenges while insisting on your capacity to handle the situation.

You may resort to avoidance, admitting your struggle but

doing nothing about it. You may assert that you can do nothing except wait it out. You may refuse to discuss it with each other, claiming that it will ultimately resolve itself.

You may use scapegoating, admitting your struggle but blaming it on work, your parents, or the stock market. Your struggle will be resolved when and if the scapegoat changes. Meanwhile, you can only bear up under it.

All three coping methods guarantee that the crisis will deepen. You cannot draw closer to God by denying that you have been feeling increasingly detached or by sitting passively in your alienation or by casting blame.

When the psalmist felt depressed and far from God, he was distressed and perplexed, but he did not fall into the traps of denial, avoidance, or scapegoating. He declared,

> As a deer longs for flowing streams,
>   so my soul longs for you, O God. . . .
> Why are you cast down, O my soul,
>   and why are you disquieted within me?
>   (Psalm 42:1, 5)

The psalmist poured out his feelings to God, who seemed almost beyond reach. And by the end of his complaint, the light of faith already was piercing the darkness of his soul:

> Hope in God; for I shall again praise him,
>   my help and my God.
>   (Psalm 42:11)

Why are such ineffective methods of dealing with crisis so

common? Primarily, we believe, because they appear to offer protection. Denial protects you from the notion that you are the kind of person (weak? immature? dependent?) who has such problems. It may also protect what you want to believe about your marriage and family: *We are happy and well-adjusted.*

Avoidance protects you from the pain of dealing with the problem. After all, if time really heals all things (actually, it doesn't), why go through the pain of working through a problem? Why not just wait it out until it goes away?

Scapegoating protects you from having to deal with a problem and also from acknowledging any personal responsibility for it. If God seems distant, it is more comforting to think that some sinister demon has intruded and disrupted the relationship rather than to think that you have somehow failed. If your spouse acts sexually cool toward you, it may be easier to blame him or her for being too immersed in other concerns rather than to ask how you might have contributed to the problem.

Protecting yourself in these ways is an instinctive reaction. Unfortunately, the protection is spurious. Denial, avoidance, and scapegoating turn out to be more destructive than protective. They tend to prolong the crisis and impede your spiritual and marital growth. How, then, can you deal with crises more effectively?

HOW TO GROW THROUGH CRISES

It isn't true that death and taxes are the only two certainties of life. You can also be certain that you will encounter crises. When you do, you will need to "be strong in the Lord and in the strength of his power" (Eph. 6:10). And the way to be strong, Paul goes on to say, is to "put on the whole armor of God, so that you may be able to stand against the wiles of the devil" (Eph. 6:11).

So be prepared. Be strong when the crisis hits. Face the crisis with resources in hand. What does this mean? Obviously, the stronger your faith and your marriage, the better equipped you are to deal with crises. Two researchers have identified eleven practices that develop the resilience families need to deal with challenges and crises:[4]

- Learn to manage your disagreements in a way that each of you finds acceptable.

- Celebrate birthdays, religious days, and other special events.

- Practice good communication.

- Stay committed to your family and have confidence that the family will survive, no matter what.

- Manage your finances well.

- Strive for good physical and emotional health.

- Engage in shared leisure activities.

- Accept one another's personality traits.

- Develop a social support network of friends and relatives.

- Eat meals together and share household chores.

- Develop your own family traditions.

These practices build your emotional capital and strengthen your marriage. The more they characterize your life, therefore, the better prepared you are to handle crises. Preparation will soften the edges of struggle and the pain of crises. It will help you deal with crises in ways that encourage you to grow through them rather than merely survive.

Further, we recommend that you take the following actions whenever a crisis occurs. Keep in mind that the more you practice them with your spouse, the more readily you will turn to them in your relationship with God and vice versa:

1. *Confront the crisis.* As we noted earlier, your first impulse may be to call upon the methods that seem to protect you—denial, avoidance, and scapegoating. Resist them, and confront the crisis. Be proactive and assertive. As Thomas à Kempis wisely wrote, "So many people are kept back from spiritual growth, and from tackling their faults in earnest, by one single fault—running away from difficulties; we don't like a tussle."[5]

Kent and Holly, whom we discussed earlier in this chapter, struggled more than necessary because Kent did not confront the loss of his job. He kept insisting that the healing power of time would eventually end the crisis, that somehow a job for him would emerge before they were hopelessly in debt. He wouldn't discuss the possibility of Holly's getting a job. He vetoed the idea, then argued with her when she continued to pursue it. Ironically, as Kent came to realize, you don't really avoid confrontation; you only delay it.

Learning this lesson also took a long time for Miriam. She spent years agonizing over her husband's drinking problem and making excuses for him. At first she accepted his denials that he had a problem and then later went along with his excuses that stress caused his drinking. Finally, her emotions wrung dry and her dream of a fulfilling marriage nearly dead, Miriam went to a therapist. The therapist helped her confront her husband. She and their children presented him with an ultimatum that they were prepared to carry out—either he stopped drinking, or he would lose his family. He broke down in tears, accepted their terms, joined Alcoholics Anonymous, and has been sober for a number of years. Miriam only regrets that she endured so many difficult and painful years before confronting her husband.

2. *Accept your Christian humanity.* We have known Christian couples who do not confront a crisis in their relationship because they are embarrassed to have one. They believe that Christians should not experience the kinds of marital problems that afflict others. But Christians are not exempt from marital crises. We are vulnerable to all the difficulties humans face. Even

Jesus, who was fully human and fully God, had to deal with temptation, opposition, disappointment, suffering, and death. He assured his disciples that they too would encounter a great deal of opposition and suffering. He also reminded them that God makes the "sun rise on the evil and on the good, and sends rain on the righteous and on the unrighteous" (Matt. 5:45). In other words, Christian or not, every person will endure storms.

Yet God also promises to be with you in those crises. No experience, no situation, no force, or anything else in all of creation can "separate us from the love of God in Christ Jesus our Lord" (Rom. 8:39). To accept your humanity is to acknowledge the fact that you will encounter crises. To accept your Christian humanity is to acknowledge that God will be with you in those crises.

Because God is at work in your marriage, you can expect to grow through the crisis. Once Kent accepted his Christian humanity, he and Holly were able to deal with their situation in a more constructive way. Kent had to accept the fact that Christian men can't always support their families. He had to revisit his ideas about his wife working. He had to reaffirm his faith that God was still with them and would help them find a way out of the morass in which they were mired. They agreed to view whatever job opportunity opened up as God's way of helping them. Holly found a job first. Eventually Kent also got work. Today both agree that their marriage is richer than it was before the crisis.

As you accept your Christian humanity and work through marital crises, you become better prepared to deal with troublesome aspects of your relationship with God, such as times when you feel you are treated unjustly, when you suffer without reason, or when the massive evil in the world assaults your faith in a loving and just God. In going through such a crisis, an individual often wonders, "Where is God?" This question implies that God should protect us from painful situations or at least that God should quickly rescue us from such situations. Again, the unsettling news is that Christians are not exempt from the adversity faced by the rest of humanity. The good news is that Christians know they are in God's hands during the difficulty.

Accepting your Christian humanity at such times is one tool for growing through a crisis rather than merely surviving it. We watched our pastor, who was struggling with a lengthy and painful illness, stand shakily in the pulpit and declare: "God is not the author of sickness." He went on to say that he didn't yet understand his illness but was confident that God would somehow use it to help him be a more effective pastor. Without a doubt he had accepted both that he was not exempt from crises and that God was at work within him during the crisis. He expected to grow through the crisis.

3. *Keep your balance: Reach out to others in need.* This principle may seem strange. After all, when you're in a crisis, the last thing that may come to mind is how you can help someone

else. The point is not that you'll stop dealing with your own crisis. Rather, it is to *maintain balance* in your life. Becoming self-absorbed during an emergency is all too easy. And self-absorbed people have two disabilities in dealing with a crisis: (1) They suffer more because their minds are fixated on their problem, and (2) They are less able to deal effectively with the crisis because they are less attuned to their world and all the resources available to them. If you or your spouse or both of you are self-absorbed, you cut yourselves off from one of your most important resources: each other.

Balancing self-concern with concern for others during a crisis can provide, in some cases, the narrow path that leads out of the wilderness of suffering. Many Christians have testified that they achieved victory over a spirit-crushing crisis by turning some of their attention to the needs of others. Consider the following examples of persons who have known the liberating experience of reaching out:

- a depressed woman who felt estranged from her husband and severed from God until she started doing volunteer work with a children's clinic;

- a couple whose child died of cancer and who worked through their feelings of alienation from each other by forming a support group for other victims;

- a man struggling with doubts about his faith who committed to ministering as though his faith were strong;

- a couple with a difference of opinion about where to live (their strong preferences were two thousand miles apart) until they undertook a ministry to homeless people in their community.

Thinking about and responding to the needs of others during a crisis is not instinctive or easy. But Jesus modeled such behavior for us. As he traveled toward Jerusalem and the Cross, he must have thought often about the ordeal that lay before him. He was immersed in his crisis. Yet when blind Bartimaeus shouted out for help, Jesus stopped to heal him (Mark 10:46-52). Even the agony of the Cross did not quench Jesus' concern for others: He forgave the penitent thief and committed his mother to the care of John. Again, it is neither instinctive nor easy to reach out to others in need when you are in crisis. But as Jesus showed, it can be done. And as many Christians can testify, it is healing to do so.

4. *Hold on to the ties that bind.* "A threefold cord is not quickly broken" (Eccles. 4:12). As we noted in the preface, we view Christian marriage as one where God, husband, and wife are securely entwined. Such a marriage nourishes the faith of each partner, and as faith deepens, the marital bond becomes even stronger.

As your ties to God and your spouse strengthen, they will increasingly serve as a source of joy in your life. They will also be the lifeline that keeps you from being swept away by the torrents of crisis. The stronger the threefold cord during a time of crisis, the better able you are to grow through the experience. So hold on to and nurture your ties.

The work and financial crisis facing Kent and Holly could have permanently ruptured their lives. It was on course to do so. Only as they renewed and reaffirmed their ties to each other and to God were they able to deal with the crisis constructively. Instead of warring with each other as well as the world, they came together and drew upon the resources of their Christian union to fight the good fight.

But you ask: What if the crisis involves my relationship with God or my spouse or both? Our answer is the same: Hold on to the ties that bind you. Let's assume you have a crisis in your relationship with God, a crisis that involves doubts about the value of prayer. Prayer is no longer meaningful to you; it seems to make no difference whether or not you pray. Your tie with God has grown weak. To stop praying, however, will only weaken it further. To continue to pray is to hold on to the tie. Use the tie with your spouse to talk about your struggle and to help you to continue a life of prayer (perhaps by praying together more). We are convinced that ultimately your persistence will strengthen your relationship with God and give you a new sense of the meaningfulness of prayer. Indeed, many Christians have experienced the "dark night of the soul" when their supplications seemed pointless, yet persistence in prayer led them to a new and higher plane of spiritual living.

Similarly, if the crisis involves your relationship with your spouse, to persist in the tie means to keep loving, talking with, and praying for him or her. In working with small groups we have listened to individuals who were deeply hurt by their spouses. The welcome news is that we also have heard about the experiences of those who said that maintaining a strong tie with God through daily prayer for the spouse and the marriage brought about a cleansing of the negative feelings.

Hold on to the ties that bind you. As long as they exist, you are not helpless or hopeless. If the ties have weakened, work to strengthen them again. Be assured that even crises, painful though they may be, can become times of growth.

FACE-TO-FACE

You can do the following activity as a couple, but we urge you to invite two or three other couples to participate with you. Give them a copy of the exercise beforehand so they can think about their responses.

In this chapter, we listed eleven practices that develop resilience (see pp. 196–97). We pointed out that the more you incorporate these practices into your life, the more prepared you are to grow through, rather than merely survive, crises. For this exercise, select any two of these practices. Then ask everyone in the group to answer the following questions about each practice:

1. What does it mean to engage in this practice?

2. In what ways does this practice reflect biblical teachings or our understanding of the meaning of being Christian?

3. What do we do now that reflects this practice?

4. What is our goal in incorporating this practice in our marriage, and how can we achieve it?

Encourage the group to make concrete plans. You also may want to plan a follow-up meeting to discuss the effectiveness of these plans in developing resilience or to explore additional practices with the same four questions.

If you choose do this exercise as a couple, follow the same procedure. You may want to discuss all eleven practices over several weeks. Take stock of how well you build them into your relationship, and make specific plans to strengthen each of them.

In your prayer time give God thanks for the ties you have, and ask God to help you to act daily in ways that strengthen those ties.

PRAY TOGETHER

O compassionate Christ, who came to make us whole, have mercy on us in our struggles and afflictions. We ask not to escape the common trials of life but to know the comfort of your presence while we are in those trials. We thank you for the promise that you work for our good in all circumstances. And so we give our struggles and afflictions to you, that you may use them to fashion us into stronger and more useful disciples. Amen.

10

Creating and Celebrating Moments of Joy

Let your fountain be blessed,
and rejoice in the wife of your youth. . . .
may you be intoxicated always by her love.

—Proverbs 5:18-19

When a woman was interviewed after winning an Olympic gold medal, the announcer said that this had to be the best day of her life. She agreed that it was indeed a great day. But, she said, it was not the best day. The best was the day she got married.

Henri Nouwen wrote that for most of his life he tended to think of God in terms of "solemnity and seriousness." But he came to realize something more: "When I think about the ways in which Jesus describes God's Kingdom, a joyful banquet is often at its center."[1] The kingdom of God, Nouwen realized, calls us to celebrate.

These two examples proclaim the potential richness of your relationship with your spouse and with God. As we discussed in the last chapter, you will have times of struggle and pain, of boredom and routine. Yet times of joy will also punctuate both of these relationships. Let's explore what joy means and how you can increase the number of joyous experiences in your marriage and in your relationship with God.

Joy Is . . .

The New Testament word *chara* can be translated "joy" or "delight." When you experience *chara*, or joy, what exactly do you feel? Is it what every other person feels? As we told you in chapter 1, several years ago we asked people to share with us their experiences of joy and to define what the feeling of joy meant to them. After analyzing more than a thousand responses, we concluded that joy is intense happiness plus something more. This "something more" varies among people. We heard such descriptions as "being intensely overwhelmed," "a spiritual awareness that something has entered your soul," "a natural high," and "a sense of being alive, of being at peace with God, with nature, with life, and with myself."

Clearly, not everyone experiences joy in the same way. Joy is always intense and exhilarating. Beyond that you may feel a deep sense of peace and well-being, a oneness with God, or any number of other things. Sometimes, as a husband pointed out, pinning down exactly what you feel may be difficult:

> An experience of joy that stands out in my mind occurred when I was in graduate school. My wife was pregnant with our first child. We were driving somewhere, and I was suddenly overwhelmed with this feeling of joy. I don't know what triggered it. We were not talking at the time, only driving along. And I can't even fully describe how I felt. I think I felt a little like I expect to feel in heaven—that everything is just the way God means for it to be.

Joy Is God's Will

We believe that God wants us to experience joy. Jesus told us to make our requests to the Father, to ask and receive "so that your joy may be complete" (John 16:24). Paul urged, "Rejoice always" (1 Thess. 5:16).

We believe, therefore, that God wills joy for us. We also believe that "rejoicing always" is a goal that will not be fully realized in this life. As we show in this chapter, you can take steps to increase the experience of joy in your life, but you cannot live in this world and feel constant joy.

We feel confident in asserting that Paul did not rejoice always. He surely did not feel joyous when he wrote to the

Corinthian church, expressing his agony over their sins. He did not feel joyous when he pleaded with Euodia and Syntyche of the Philippian church to stop their bickering. He must have grieved that two women who had struggled with him in the work of the gospel were now at odds with each other. In various other letters he wrote about his anxieties and frustrations with the churches. There is no joy in these words.

Like Paul, you will not experience joy in every circumstance. How can you encounter suffering and oppression and feel joyous? We have often heard Christians who left the comfort of home to minister to the desperate tell of the turmoil and pain they experienced in the face of spirit-crushing circumstances. Yes, they experienced joyous moments as well, but the joy was an irregular gift rather than a constant theme.

In the face of the difficulties of life, how do you maximize the joy in your relationship with each other and with God? Knowing that God wills for you to be joyful, how do you increase the number of your joyous moments?

Joy Is Both Cause and Effect

To increase joy in your life, you must recognize its sources. What causes joy? In our tabulation of experiences of joy, we found relationships mentioned as the most frequent source, including the relationship with God and spouse. Individuals with strong ties to God and spouse experienced joy in these relationships.

As you cultivate ever-closer bonds with God and spouse, then, your joy will increase measurably. You will be able to say to God the words of the psalmist: "You show me the path of life. / In your presence there is fullness of joy; / in your right hand are pleasures forevermore" (Ps. 16:11). You will be able to affirm to each other the uplifting wisdom of Proverbs 5:18-19: "Rejoice in the wife of your youth, . . . may you be intoxicated always by her love." You will discover that your intoxication with each other can last beyond the flush of the early days of your marriage, remaining until death do you part. Theodore Roosevelt made this point in a letter he wrote to a friend. He asserted that nothing in the world, no achievement of any kind, could compare with "the happiness that comes to those fortunate enough to make a real love match—a match in which lover and sweetheart will never be lost in husband and wife."[2]

Strong, meaningful ties with God and your spouse, then, will be sources of joyous experiences throughout your life. Joy is not only the effect of those ties but also their cause. Every shared joyous experience strengthens the ties because joy is contagious. The more joy you share with your spouse, the closer you will feel to each other, the better you will feel about your relationship with God, and the more you will open yourself to joyous spiritual experiences. And the more joy you gain in your walk with God, the stronger and more joyous both your faith and your marriage become. Joy, in essence, strengthens your ties, and stronger ties bring more experiences of joy. You find yourself caught up in a spiral of ever more abundant life because joyous ties are increasingly the theme of your lives.

Furthermore, the good news is that you can take concrete steps to create more moments of joy in your relationships with God and spouse. There are, however, obstacles to the task.

OBSTACLES TO JOY

We have already mentioned one obstacle: the nature of the world in which we live. It's difficult to rejoice when your spouse or child gets ill, when a friend is struggling with an abusive mate, or when you see pictures of starving children. Such experiences can quench your joy. Fortunately, few people are surrounded by relentless suffering. There are times of respite even for those nearest to the heart of the world's pain.

Two other obstacles are more subtle: the fact that sources of joy are also sources of risk and challenge, and the fact that our culture continually misleads us.

Sources of Joy Are Also Sources of Risk and Challenge

You can find joy in being creative. Perhaps you have always admired oil painting, and you decide to accept the challenge and try it. Yet such an effort is always a risk. You may discover that you have talent and experience the joy of being creative. You may also discover that you have no talent and experience the gloom of failure.

Similarly, while relationships are a prime source of joy, they also involve challenge and risk. The fear of commitment that makes some people hesitate to get married reflects an intuitive awareness of the challenge and risk involved. There are no guarantees. The marriage may not work out. Even if it does, it will involve times of pain, of effort, of struggle. As a young woman put it: "I've got all I can handle with my career right now. I don't have the energy for dealing with a home and husband." We agreed with her. She was obviously not ready to take on the challenge of building a meaningful marriage.

People who do take the risk can successfully meet the challenge by persevering through the difficult and troubled times and by guarding and nurturing their relationship. They will reap a harvest of joyous experiences in the process. They will achieve the goal set forth in Proverbs—a lifelong intoxication with each other's love.

When you take the risk and meet the challenge of marriage, you are better prepared to do the same in your relationship with God. For example, when our church encouraged members to start family devotions in their homes, one husband in our couples group said, "I don't see how we could possibly do it. Between our work and the kids' activities, we hardly have time to breathe." Further discussion revealed that he did have discretionary time. He and his wife watched several television programs regularly, and their children usually had free time after they finished their homework.

The husband didn't lack time; he just didn't want to change

his lifestyle. Plus, he didn't want the additional task of leading family devotions. He was not convinced that he would gain sufficient spiritual benefits to make the effort worthwhile. We didn't offer him easy words of comfort. We agreed that he might well miss a favorite television program at times and that he would be assuming an additional task. Moreover, family devotions might not always be enjoyable, easy, or even spiritually productive.

Nevertheless, we told him that in the long run a deeper commitment would yield a harvest of joyous experiences. He had taken the risk and accepted the challenge in committing himself to his wife. He knew the joy his marriage brought. He and his wife could work together, supporting each other, as they increased their spiritual commitment. The result would be a greater measure of joy and stronger ties with each other and with God.

Our Culture Seduces Us

If joy is the destination, what's the quickest route to get there? Answers abound in our culture. Popular books and magazines market the joy of such things as having sex, cooking, riding horses, playing hockey, being good to yourself, and building high self-esteem.

The advertisements that saturate our culture lure those hungry for joy. They tap into the appeal of what author Albert Haase calls the eight golden calves of the present era: power, prestige, people, possessions, productivity, popularity, pleasure, and position: "These 'eight P's' are the 'it' we need to be happy. Without the 'eight P's,' we're nothing. We're failures. And so, like Adam and Eve, we keeping reaching out to pluck these 'eight P's,' convinced they will bring us happiness and peace."[3]

Money plays an important part in "plucking" the eight P's. As Tony Campolo notes, if you really believe the ads, you will agree that "everything needed for spiritual well-being can be secured if we just have enough money."[4] If you're not convinced, pay attention to the language used: "You deserve a break," "Something you can believe in," "It doesn't get any better than this," "The real thing," and so on.

Despite the allure of advertising language, those who get seduced by the promises and hopes of our consumer culture are deflected from the most important sources of joyous experiences. Perhaps they believe the slogan we have seen on car bumpers—"The one with the most toys wins"—rather than the teaching of Jesus: "One's life does not consist in the abundance of possessions" (Luke 12:15). In any case, it's easy to be deflected when the voices of advertisers impinge on you at every step and when people you know and respect appear to accept the message of those voices.

We would like to add a word of caution here. We do not mean to rail against possessions as though they were inherently unchristian. We are not saying that such things as a longed-for new car, a special dinner at a gourmet restaurant, or a state-of-the-art sound system won't bring you pleasure and perhaps a degree of joy. If poverty were a virtue, the Bible would have no reason to exhort us hundreds of times to care for the needs of the poor. If the lack of possessions is a more godly state, the early church made a mistake by sharing all things so that no one would lack basic needs. It is not possessions as such, but the love of possessions, the obsession with possessions, and the expectation that possessions will lead us to the highest realms of joy that must be rejected.

You can resist the seductions of the culture in two ways. First, accept the fact that the more you have, the greater your responsibility will be to share with those who do not have (you will find this to be a source of joy). Second, in the face of all the allurements that surround you, make God and your family the first priorities in your life.

CREATING MORE JOY IN YOUR LIFE

Joy is not something that just happens. There is no formula for calling up a joyous experience at will, but you can create conditions in which joyous experiences are more likely to occur.

Nurture Your Marriage

The important word here is *nurture*. We prefer it to the more common expression "work at your marriage" because working at a relationship sounds less appealing and less intrinsically rewarding. Every nurturing effort will not necessarily be fun, but it will sow the seeds of joy in your life.

Marriage does not guarantee that you will experience joy. Those persons who reap the joy of marriage are the ones who strive to make their ties stronger and more meaningful. You can nurture your marriage by thinking positive thoughts about your spouse, praying for him or her, sharing your thoughts and feelings, or by working through a disagreement in a way that satisfies both of you. Nurturing does not happen just in the lengthy and special times you are together. As Holly put it, it occurs every time something happens that makes you feel good about each other:

> When you ask me about nurturing, I think of all the little things that happen day in and day out that make us feel good about each other. When my husband holds the car door open for me even after more than twenty years of marriage. When he tells me I look good. When he interrupts something he's doing to help me get dinner ready. When he talks with me about something he's struggling with at work and tells me how much he values my opinion. Every day he does things for me that make me feel good about myself and about our marriage. That's what I call nurturing!

Nurture Your Spiritual Life

Again, the important word is *nurture*. The mere fact of being a Christian is not enough. We have known people who say they are Christians but derive no joy from their faith. They cling to their faith but do nothing to nurture it. A poorly nurtured faith, like a taken-for-granted marriage, does not result in joy.

Regular spiritual exercises, such as prayer and worship, nurture faith. When a couple shares these activities, they experience a double blessing because they nurture both their spiritual life and their marriage. Joy will not happen every time spouses pray or worship together, but these spiritual practices can be potent sources of joy. Gloria, a university professor and busy mother, told us of her reluctance to attend church one Sunday morning. "I really hadn't been getting much from the services and thought that staying home would be more beneficial," she said. However, her husband insisted, so she went. As she listened to the words and music, she was caught up in the sense of God's presence:

> It seemed as if every cell in my body stood at attention. It felt like I was being personally addressed. As I continued to worship, all the issues that had been plaguing me came into a new perspective. I experienced insight, a clarity of vision that I had never had before. . . . It brought me an overwhelming sense of exhilaration, and, at the same time, peace and well-being.

The experience not only gave her spiritual joy but also caused her to rejoice in her husband for his persistence.

Similarly, a couple who had just moved reported:

> Finally one Sunday we walked into the church we now attend. Almost from the moment we entered, we had a strong sense of God's presence. The hymns touched us. The

pastor's message was relevant to our lives. The music of the choir was inspiring. We had found our church home.

The same couple told us that they have recurring experiences of joy in worship. By nurturing their spiritual lives, they have opened themselves to joy.

Involve Yourself in the Moment

"I tend to get absorbed in my own thoughts," a man told us. "And I know that I have missed a lot. I'm trying to be less inward and more aware of what's going on around me. The more I succeed, the more joy I get out of life."

Instead of just being present in your environment, engage yourself with your surroundings. Pay attention to what is happening in the moment. Norm told us about a joyous experience while reading a bedtime story to his daughter. Rather than reading the story by rote, with his mind drifting back and forth between the story and other matters, he read with feeling and watched each expression that came to his daughter's face. He was totally involved in the moment with his daughter, and it became a memorable experience of joy for him.

Giving full attention to anything for an extended period of time is not easy for us. A religion professor told us that some Buddhist monks practice until they can focus their thoughts on an object such as a pencil for forty minutes or more. Try focusing on a pencil without letting other thoughts distract you, and you'll appreciate the monks' achievement. If you are able to focus for more than a few minutes, you are extraordinary.

Like the monks, however, you can learn to become more involved with the moment by practicing with your spouse. Whenever possible, give your spouse your full attention. We have observed three common ways that couples relate. We call them the front-to-back, side-to-side, and face-to-face modes of relating. In the front-to-back style, the husband and wife are in the same vicinity but not attending to each other (for example, the man who is three feet ahead of his wife as they are walking somewhere). In the side-to-side style, the spouses are close together but not engaged with each other (for example, the couple in a restaurant who appear like two strangers sitting at the same table). In the face-to-face style, the husband and wife are engaged with each other (for example, they talk or indicate nonverbally, perhaps by holding hands, that they are connected). This face-to-face style generates joy. As often as you can, focus on each other as you did when you were courting. If stray thoughts intrude, resist them. It's a wonderfully affirming experience to have another person give himself or herself totally to you. The more you do this for each other, the more joy you will have in your marriage.

Jason, married for more than twenty years, talks about the gains of being attentive:

> If you ask me about joy in my marriage, I have to say that the times I had joy were the times I was being attentive to my wife. When I really listen to what she's saying, when I watch her and talk to her instead of withdrawing into my own con-

cerns, when we discuss things we could do together—those are the times that I rejoice in her.

As you learn how to give your full attention to your spouse, apply it to your relationship with God. When you worship, try to focus on God. Instead of letting your mind roam among the various concerns of your life, work at staying focused on what God is saying to you, on what you want to say to God, and on what you can learn about being a more effective Christian. The more you are involved in the moment with God, the more joy you will experience in your faith.

Give Yourself to What Matters

"What will it profit them to gain the whole world and forfeit their life?" (Mark 8:36). In these words, Jesus urges you to make a cost-benefit analysis when you decide to what you will devote yourself. What really matters most in the long run? What will bring you the most joy?

As we noted earlier, you may have to go against the allurements of the culture in order to gain that which is most profitable. In the 1990s, a movement began among some Americans to simplify their lives by cutting back on their possessions and opting out of consuming careers. They decided that the race for professional or financial success zapped the time and energy needed for relationships and personal growth.

Does this mean that you should do the same? Should you abandon your present work and forego the purchase of a home computer in order to spend more time with God and with each other? We don't know. Only you can answer the question of what you need to do to give yourselves to that which benefits you the most. Some couples can pursue demanding careers and still maintain a close walk with God and with each other. Others can't. Your calling is to forge a life in which Christ dwells richly in each of you and your love for each other continues to intoxicate you both. Give yourselves to whatever pursuits enable you to fulfill that calling, and you will reap ever more joy.

Keep a Record of Joyous Experiences

Remembering a joyous time is a way to reexperience some of the joy you felt at the time. A husband told us that one of his most memorable times of joy occurred when he and his wife vacationed at a seaside cottage. He was just watching her straighten up the kitchen when a sense of joy overwhelmed him: "I was so thankful that God brought us together. Every time I think about that moment, I get a little twinge of joy."

As long as they stay alive in your memory, joyous experiences continue to enrich you. To gain the most from past experiences, keep a record of them. We suggest that you use your couple's journal to record as many joyous experiences from the past as you can recall. Then continue writing down your shared experiences of joy as they occur. Describe the circumstances and how each of you felt at the time. Get in the habit of periodically reviewing these moments. And don't forget to relive them as part of your anniversary celebration each year.

Watch the Small Things

Henri Nouwen wrote about a friend who "is so deeply connected with God that he can see joy where I expect only sadness."[5] The friend looks for joy wherever he goes and finds it in the small things that others overlook. Even in the midst of injustice or need in another country, he encounters a child or a couple or a scene of some sort in which he sees the hand of God. And this brings him joy.

So watch for evidence of the hand of God in small, everyday things. See God at work in the look of affection your spouse gives you. Share with your spouse the handiwork of God in a beautiful sunset. Joy is to be found not just in the dramatic, but in the small things of life. Recall Jason, who experienced joy when he was attentive to his wife: "Sometimes I just look at her talking to someone at a party or walking down the street to meet me for lunch, and I feel joy."

Practice Gratitude

In our experience, joyous people are invariably grateful people as well. Gratitude is fertile ground for the growth of joy. It's impossible to feel grateful without experiencing at least a twinge of joy.

To create more joy, therefore, we need to practice gratitude. Notice that we do not say to "be grateful." The *feeling* of gratitude is not one that you can control. The *practice* of gratitude, on the other hand, is. The more you practice gratitude, the more you feel it; the more you feel it, the more you will rejoice.

You can practice gratitude by doing what an old gospel hymn urges: "Count your blessings, name them one by one." Whatever your circumstances, you can always find something to be grateful for, such as the fact that you are God's children and that you have each other. Give God thanks in prayer. Regularly express thanksgiving for your marriage. Review your day, and express thanks to God and your spouse for every blessing. Tell each other regularly the things about your relationship for which you are grateful. Your gratitude will lead you to joy.

Engage in Ministry

Mother Teresa told an assembled group that she and they were all pencils that God can use to write love letters to the world. It's a wonderful image, an image of ministry. Engaging in ministry is a wonderful privilege that reaps a greater harvest of joy.

We believe that every Christian is called to some kind of ministry. Your task is to find and participate in the ministry to which God is calling you. You and your spouse can share in that ministry. At the very least, you can tell each other what you are doing and pray for each other. Even more, you may be able to work as partners in some area of ministry. We have seen the joy in couples who have labored together in such ministries as teaching Sunday school, participating in lay mission projects, leading youth programs, and working with poor and homeless people. We have often experienced it ourselves.

One of our experiences involved leading a marriage support group at our church. When we learned about the need for such a group, we volunteered. Even though we were heavily involved with university teaching at the time, we felt called to this work. We anticipated that the group would meet once a month on Sunday. We thought that putting together a monthly program on a day when we were already at church would not be burdensome.

At the first meeting, however, the couples agreed unanimously that they wanted to meet every week on Wednesday evening. We suddenly faced a great deal more work and inconvenience than we had anticipated. But we had made the commitment. So for a number of years we met with the group weekly. Admittedly, on many Wednesday evenings after working all day, we drove the thirty minutes to church with considerable reluctance. Invariably, we drove the thirty minutes back home feeling elated! Our work with the group brought us an untold number of joyous memories and many close friends. And because we worked together, the ministry enriched our own relationship immeasurably.

Keep Trying

Someone once said that a saint is a sinner who keeps trying. And then there's the old story of the snail who was inching up the trunk of a cherry tree. A beetle stuck its head out of a hole and told the snail it was wasting its time because there were no cherries on the tree. The snail replied, "There will be by the time I get there."

The point is obvious: Good things come to those who per-severe. If you follow all the principles and don't reap a quick harvest of joyous experiences, persevere. Eventually the joy will come. It will come because it is God's will and God's promise.

Face-to-Face

Gratitude that is felt and openly expressed is a major source of joy. Talk about persons for whom you are grateful—those who have enriched you as individuals or as a couple. They may be persons you know well or those who unknowingly had a major impact on your life. Make a list, and write letters of gratitude. Write separate letters to those who enriched you as individuals and joint letters to those who enriched you as a couple.

Don't forget to include your spouse on this list and to write each other a letter. Tell your spouse about many ways he or she has enriched your life, and recall experiences you have shared that put a glow in your heart when you think of them. After you read your letters to each other, spend some time talking about this exercise. How did it make you feel to write to people who have enriched you? How often did you experience joy? How did you feel about writing to your spouse and receiving a letter from your spouse? Did you write about similar experiences? How much did your spouse's recollection of shared experiences surprise you? What do the letters tell you about ways to increase the joy in your marriage?

In your prayer time, thank God for the people to whom you wrote. Ask God to bless them. Give thanks for each other, and ask God to nurture your marriage so that you may rejoice with each other and in each other throughout your life together.

PRAY TOGETHER

We praise you, God, for you are the source of every good and perfect gift. We praise you, Christ, for you have promised us a joy that nothing can take from us. We praise you, Holy Spirit, for you dwell within us to reap a harvest of abundance. We thank you, triune God, for making us one flesh. We ask you to continue to nurture our marriage so that we may, in accordance with your will, rejoice with each other and in each other throughout our life together. In your holy name we pray. Amen.

NOTES

Chapter 1

1. Robert H. Lauer and Jeanette C. Lauer, *Marriage and Family: The Quest for Intimacy*, 4th ed. (New York: McGraw-Hill, 2000), 17–18.
2. Madeleine L'Engle, *Penguins and Golden Calves: Icons and Idols* (Wheaton, Ill.: Harold Shaw Publishers, 1996), 98.
3. Thomas Merton, *No Man Is an Island* (New York: Harcourt Brace Jovanovich, 1955), 152.
4. Kathleen Norris, *The Quotidian Mysteries: Laundry, Liturgy, and "Women's Work"* (New York: Paulist Press, 1998), 70.

Chapter 2

1. William James, *Psychology* (New York: Henry Holt and Co., 1905), 179.
2. John Powell, *Why Am I Afraid to Tell You Who I Am?: Insights into Personal Growth* (Allen, Tex.: Tabor Publishing, 1969), 11.
3. Jeanette C. Lauer and Robert H. Lauer, *No Secrets?: How Much Honesty Is Good for Your Marriage?* (Grand Rapids, Mich.: Zondervan Publishing House, 1993), 203–15.
4. Ken Gire, *Windows of the Soul: Experiencing God in New Ways* (Grand Rapids, Mich.: Zondervan Publishing House, 1996), 104.
5. Ibid.

Chapter 3

1. Lewis Carroll, *Alice's Adventures in Wonderland and Through the Looking-Glass* (New York: New American Library, 1960), 26.
2. Paul Tournier, *The Meaning of Persons* (New York: Harper & Row, 1957), 83.
3. See Calvin S. Hall, *A Primer of Freudian Psychology* (New York: New American Library, 1954), for a discussion of defense mechanisms from a Freudian viewpoint.

4. Philip Yancey, *Reaching for the Invisible God: What Can We Expect to Find?* (Grand Rapids, Mich.: Zondervan Publishing House, 2000), 45.

Chapter 4

1. Edward Hays, *The Ladder: Parable Stories of Ascension and Descension* (Leavenworth, Kans.: Forest of Peace Publishing, 1999), 52.
2. Thomas Merton, *New Seeds of Contemplation* (New York: New Directions, 1972), 47.
3. Gordon W. Allport, *Becoming: Basic Considerations for a Psychology of Personality* (New Haven, Conn.: Yale University Press, 1955), 66.
4. *The Wisdom of the Desert: Sayings from the Desert Fathers of the Fourth Century,* translated by Thomas Merton (New York: New Directions, 1970), 57.
5. Wendy M. Wright, *The Rising: Living the Mysteries of Lent, Easter, and Pentecost* (Nashville, Tenn.: Upper Room Books, 1994), 139.
6. Thomas à Kempis, *The Imitation of Christ,* translated by Ronald Knox and Michael Oakley (London: Burns & Oates, 1959), 74.

Chapter 5

1. Mother Teresa, *Total Surrender,* edited by Brother Angelo Devananda (Ann Arbor, Mich.: Servant Publications, 1985), 63.
2. Saint Bernard, *On the Love of God* (New York: Morehouse-Gorham, 1950), 44.
3. *The Autobiography of Saint Thérèse of Lisieux: The Story of a Soul,* translated by John Beevers (New York: Image Books, 1957), 147.
4. Robert H. Lauer and Jeanette C. Lauer, *The Joy Ride: Everyday Ways to Lasting Happiness* (Nashville, Tenn.: Dimensions for Living, 1994), 132.
5. Susan Johnson with Hara Estroff Marano, "Love: The Immutable Longing for Contact," *Psychology Today* (March–April 1994): 32–37.
6. Michael Downey, "Making a Way," *Weavings: A Journal of the Christian Spiritual Life* 9:4 (July–August 1994): 15.
7. *Early Christian Fathers,* vol. 1, edited by Cyril C. Richardson (London: SCM Press, 1953), 152.

8. Paul Brand and Philip Yancey, *Fearfully and Wonderfully Made* (Grand Rapids, Mich.: Zondervan Publishing House, 1987), 139.

Chapter 6
1. Charles Dickens, *Bleak House* (New York: New American Library, 1964), 116.
2. Ibid., 117.
3. Thomas Merton, *Life and Holiness* (New York: Image Books, 1963), 116.

Chapter 7
1. Robert Rosenthal and Lenore Jacobson, *Pygmalion in the Classroom: Teacher Expectation and Pupils' Intellectual Development* (New York: Holt, Rinehart and Winston, 1968).
2. Virginia Satir, *Peoplemaking* (Palo Alto, Calif.: Science and Behavior Books, 1972), 27.
3. Aaron T. Beck, M.D., *Love Is Never Enough: How Couples Can Overcome Misunderstandings, Resolve Conflicts, and Solve Relationship Problems through Cognitive Therapy* (New York: Harper & Row, 1989), 197.
4. à Kempis, *Imitation of Christ,* 17.

Chapter 8
1. Viktor E. Frankl, *Man's Search for Meaning: An Introduction to Logotherapy,* translated by Ilse Lasch (New York: Pocket Books, 1963), 61.
2. Ibid., 64.
3. Erich Fromm, *Psychoanalysis and Religion* (New Haven, Conn.: Yale University Press, 1950), 86–87.
4. William Barclay, *Flesh and Spirit: An Examination of Galatians 5:19-23* (London: SCM Press, 1962), 63 ff.
5. Jeanette C. Lauer and Robert H. Lauer, *Til Death Do Us Part: A Study and Guide to Long-Term Marriage* (New York: Harrington Park Press, 1986), 179.
6. Morton Kelsey, *Set Your Hearts on the Greatest Gift: Living the Art of Christian Love* (Nashville: Upper Room Books, 1996), 12 ff.
7. Ibid., 19.

8. *Charles de Foucauld: Writings Selected with an Introduction by Robert Ellsburg* (Maryknoll, N.Y.: Orbis Books, 1999), 87.
9. Ibid.

Chapter 9

1. Beck, *Love Is Never Enough*, 74.
2. Søren Kierkegaard, *Edifying Discourses: A Selection*, edited by Paul L. Holmer and translated by David F. and Lillian Marvin Swenson (New York: Harper & Brothers Publishers, 1958), 183.
3. Helmut Thielicke, *The Waiting Father: Sermons on the Parables of Jesus*, translated by John W. Doberstein (London: James Clarke & Co., 1960), 47.
4. Hamilton I. McCubbin and Marilyn A. McCubbin, "Typologies of Resilient Families: Emerging Roles of Social Class and Ethnicity," *Family Relations* 37 (July 1988): 247–54.
5. à Kempis, *Imitation of Christ*, 57.

Chapter 10

1. Henri J. M. Nouwen, *The Return of the Prodigal Son: A Story of Homecoming* (New York: Image Books, 1994), 113.
2. Edward Wagenknecht, *The Seven Worlds of Theodore Roosevelt* (New York: Longmans, Green & Co., 1958), 165.
3. Albert Haase, *Swimming in the Sun: Discovering the Lord's Prayer with Francis of Assisi and Thomas Merton* (Cincinnati, Ohio: St. Anthony Messenger Press, 1993), 176.
4. Tony Campolo, *Carpe Diem: Seize the Day* (Dallas, Tex.: Word Publishing, 1995), 44.
5. Nouwen, *Return of the Prodigal Son*, 115.

ABOUT THE AUTHORS

Married in 1954, Robert and Jeanette Lauer have three children and five grandchildren. They have written fifteen books and numerous articles for religious and popular magazines. The Lauers speak from their experience in counseling and working with couples in marriage enrichment groups for many years.

Robert holds B.S. and Ph.D. degrees from Washington University, St. Louis, Missouri, and a B.D. from Southern Baptist Theological Seminary, Louisville, Kentucky. Jeanette holds a B.S. degree from the University of Missouri, St. Louis, and a Ph.D. from Washington University. Both served as professors and deans at U.S. International University.

Don't miss these Upper Room titles

Parents and Grandparents As Spiritual Guides
by Betty Shannon Cloyd

From the beginning God has commanded us to be spiritual companions for our children and grandchildren. In *Parents and Grandparents As Spiritual Guides*, Betty Cloyd explores the ways in which parents and grandparents can introduce children to the presence of God and nurture them spiritually during routine daily activities, as well as in planned devotional times.
ISBN 0-8358-0923-4 • Paperback •168 pages

The Christ-Centered Woman
Finding Balance in a World of Extremes
by Kimberly Dunnam Reisman

Christian women must respond to many callings—those of family and home, work and colleagues, ministry and discipleship. In this insightful guide, Kimberly Dunnam Reisman confronts the daily chaos of competing demands from a new perspective. Instead of asking, "How do I juggle all my responsibilities?" she asks, "How do I make choices that reflect my relationship with Christ and Christ's direction for my life?" *The Christ-Centered Woman* identifies barriers to balanced living and reveals how being centered in the Savior can help us contemplate, sort, and prioritize our callings.

ISBN 0-8358-0913-7 • Paperback • 112 pages

At Home with God
by Anne Broyles, Sue Downing, Paul Escamilla, Elizabeth Lind Escamilla, and Marilyn Brown Oden

Drawing closer to God as a family is often an easier desire to express than a practical reality. Parents want to nurture their children in a growing relationship with God and to help their children develop daily devotional practices. Despite that desire, we are often caught in the grip of a scheduling vise. *At Home with God* features brief, daily family devotions that can be used throughout the school year. The book is planned especially for families with children ages six to twelve.

ISBN 0-8358-0933-1 • Paperback • 325 pages